The Story of West Carbery

THE FRIENDLY PRESS

Published 1985
by
THE FRIENDLY PRESS
61 Newtown Road
Waterford

Typeset: Century
10 on 13 point.

Printed by
Litho Press
Roxboro Mews,
Midleton
Co. Cork

ISBN: 0-948728-00-0

CONTENTS

ILLUSTRATIONS

Cover picture shows River Ilen with road bridge in front of and railway bridge behind West Cork Hotel. (circa 1910)

FOREWORD

My uncle, William John Kingston, was born in Skibbereen in 1885, younger son of William Kingston and Sarah Anne Kingston (nee Wolfe). He was educated at his sisters' school in Skibbereen. He then qualified as a Solicitor and was awarded a Gold Medal and Findlater Scholarship by the Incorporated Law Society in 1906. He travelled widely, practising in South Africa during the early 1920s, but joined his cousin Jasper Wolfe in 1926 and from then until his final retirement, practised in Skibbereen in the firm of J. Travers Wolfe.

He was a keen historian and archaeologist and was frequently consulted by those seeking information on local history and genealogy. In the 1940s he was one of the founders of the Skibbereen Archaeological Society and for many years helped to arrange field outings and lectures. His long legal experience gave him insights into the history and customs of the locality and he told many an entertaining story with a strong, but kindly, sense of humour.

The Story of West Carbery was completed in 1948 and readers are asked to bear this in mind in any allusions to this century. It has been felt right to leave the text exactly as he wrote it. The time lag may be explained by the fact that he did not wish it published until after his death. He died in 1975.

—Daisy L. Swanton

William J. Kingston

The Story of
West Carbery

CHAPTER I

Our story commences at the dawn of history when fact and fiction are as much interwoven as they are in War Communiques!

We are told that there were 3 early invasions of Ireland from the Continent, via England, first by the pastoral Firbolgs, who were conquered by the magical and warlike Danaans about 1000 B.C., who, in their turn, were conquered by the Milesians about 500 B.C.

The first two invaders belonged to the Bronze Age, but it was the Milesians who introduced iron and the Celtic speech.

It is related that Nuada the last of the Danaan's chieftains said to the conquering Milesians:—

"We give you Ireland, but since our hands have fashioned it we will not utterly leave the country. We will be in the white mist that clings to the mountains; we will be in the quiet that broods on the lakes; we will be in the joy shout of the rivers; we will be in the secret wisdom of the woods. Long after your descendants have forgotten us they will hear our music on sunny raths, and see our great white horses lift their heads from the mountain tarns and shake the night dew from their crested manes; in the end they will know that all the beauty in the world comes back to us and their battles are only the echo of ours."

We are also told that two brothers Heber and Heremon (sons of Milesius who was then dead) were in command of the Milesians, and that they were accompanied by their relative Lug Ith, the son of Ith, who was himself an uncle of Milesius. After this conquest the remaining Firbolgs were given the same choice as the Irish, 2000 years later, got from Cromwell, i.e. between Hell and Connaught! Then the conquerors divided Ireland between themselves and Heber took Munster, save that Lug Ith got Corca Laidhe (the marshy territory), including the modern Baronies of Carbery, Bear and Bantry. Then came the usual sequel, Heber (encouraged by his wife) claimed he had been unfairly treated in the division and he attacked Heremon, but was defeated and slain, and Heremon became sole King of Ireland. Lug Ith, however, does not seem to have been disturbed, and he was the progenitor of the O'Driscolls who, at one time, owned the whole of Corca Laidhe, stretching from the Kenmare River to the Bandon River.

Before the Norman invasion, of which we shall speak later, there was a King O'Driscoll, who had under him 7 chiefs, each ruling over a specified district (Tuath), equivalent roughly to about a modern Civil Parish, and under these chiefs there were 71 hereditary leaders, being the heads of landowning families, so the O'Driscolls were a power in the land in those days. But, as centuries rolled by, they lost most of their territory owing to invasions of other Irish tribes.

First came the O'Mahonys, who were located at Kinalmeaky (Bandon). About 450 A.D. we find them, under their chief Cas, in possession of that part of Corca Laidhe called Ivagha (the western land), comprising then the Parishes of Kilmoe, Schull, Kilcrohane, Durrus, Caheragh and Kilmocomogue, so their territory, at that time, including Kinalmeaky, stretched from Cork to the Mizzen Head, and from the River Lee to the northern boundary of what was left of Corca Laidhe, and corresponded roughly to the Diocese of Cork. Both the O'Driscolls and the O'Mahonys were subject to the King of Cashel.

The next Irish invaders were the powerful McCarthy

clan who, coming from Tipperary about the time of the Norman invasion (1170), captured Cork, Kinsale etc. from the O'Mahonys. The McCarthys, who claimed descent from Heber, became later subdivided, McCarthy Mor ruling in East Cork and McCarthy Reagh (swarthy) ruling over Carbery, of which Donal Gott (meaning stammerer) McCarthy became overlord in 1232. His great-grandson, another Donal, was the first to be called Reagh, and he succeeded as chief by murdering his uncle. This latter branch continued to expand until, at the opening of the 16th century, McCarthy Reagh was overlord from Bantry Bay to the Bandon River, and half of Carbery (including land in and round Skibbereen and Kilcoe) was either in his hands as demesne lands or in those of subordinate McCarthy septs, such as Clan Dermod and Clan Teighe, founded by two sons of Donal Gott. There is practically no information to show how the McCarthys became possessed of such large estates and influence in County Cork in which they owned nothing before the Norman conquest, nor what became of the earlier inhabitants, nor what reward the McCarthy soldiers got for conquering the territory, but, as many of these soldiers were kinsmen of the two chiefs, presumably they did not do badly. At that rough time, when territory was conquered, it was customary to drive out, or kill, or enslave, the previous inhabitants and the conqueror then divided up the captured land between his sons and near relatives. But though the McCarthy's rise to power was quick and widespread their collapse, as we shall see later, was as quick and complete. After the arrival of the McCarthys the O'Driscoll territory was reduced to the portion between Courtmacsherry and Roaring Water Bay and the Bear peninsula, corresponding roughly to the Protestant Diocese of Ross.

The next invading tribe to arrive in Carbery were the O'Donovans, who came from Limerick about 1178 (or perhaps a little later), and they were old allies of the

O'Mahonys. They secured for themselves a strip of land running from Bantry to Glandore. About the same time the O'Learys, who had been located on the sea coast between Ross and Glandore, moved off to Inchigeela, probably squeezed out between the McCarthys and the O'Donovans, and the latter extended themselves eastwards to the Roury River.

Finally the O'Sullivans moved from Tipperary to Kerry about 1192 and later captured the Baronies of Bear and Bantry.

These various movements had the effect of cutting the O'Mahony territory in two, and so from about 1200 there were different chiefs for Ivagha and Kinalmeaky. Furthermore, the O'Driscoll territory had shrunk to a strip of land running from Castlehaven to Roaring Water Bay, including the islands off the coast.

But the O'Driscoll seaboard must have produced a good revenue for them, as, from an Inquisition of 1609, we get a list of dues levied by them on all boats from The Fastnet to Toe Head. These Inquisitions, which were something like our Coroner's Inquests, were customary at that time to enquire into the property and heirs of persons of importance and were taken before Jurors. It would be too long to set out here all the dues but there are a few examples:—

"Every ship or boat that fisheth there is to pay to the Lord in money 19s.2d., a barrel of flour, a barrel of salt, a hogshead of beer, and a dish of fish 3 times a week from every boat, viz. Wed., Fri. and Sat., and if they dry their fish in any part of the country they are to pay 13/- for the rocks. That if any boat of them do chance to take a halibut they must give it to the Lord for a ball of butter and if they conceal it from him for 24 hours they forfeit 40/- to the Lord. That for every beef they kill they pay 8d. and for every pig and sheep that is killed they pay a penny."

Besides, any person who should pilot a ship above 10

tons through the North West passage out of Baltimore without a special licence from The O'Driscoll was liable to pay him a fine of £5., and any person boarding a ship coming into Baltimore Harbour, without first obtaining The O'Driscoll's permission, had to pay a fine of £1. 6. 8. In addition every ship paid 4d. for anchorage dues, and if any wine was landed the Lord took 4 gallons out of a butt, and if he bought wine he got a reduction of 2d. per gallon. The fishermen of the country paid much reduced dues. The Lord bought fish 2d. per dozen less than ordinary price. He also got the first offer of all goods brought by sea and of all goods sold by the freeholders of his country. The latter, however, got paid therefor at current prices, but outside traders got less.

The O'Mahonys and O'Donovans also collected dues for their portions of the coast. During these centuries large numbers of Spanish, Portuguese, French and Belgian ships came to our waters to fish and trade so the chiefs must have collected considerable revenues from them.

After the 4 great tribes of West Carbery had got settled down in their new quarters, even though there were sporadic outbreaks between them, still there were also many intermarriages.

It was only about 1000 A.D. that it became fashionable to adopt and use a surname as, hitherto, when population was sparse, Christian names sufficed, which were often of a descriptive nature, or as we should say, nicknames. The O'Driscoll surname comes from "Eiderscel" who flourished about 950 A.D. It means "descendant of interpreter" and it would be interesting to know how this arose. O'Mahony means "descendant of Mahon", one of their chiefs who died about 1038 A.D. McCarthy means "son of Carthagh" and O'Donovan "descendant of Donovan", also derived from their chiefs.

Very little about Ireland seems to have been known by

the Mediterranean nations at the beginning of the Christian era. For example, the Greek geographer, Strabo, writing about 20 A.D., stated that Ireland was at the very skirt of the habitable world, and was scarcely suitable for human settlement, and that the natives were cannibals.

Again in 43 A.D. Mela, a Spaniard, stated that he heard "Ivernia" could not ripen corn, but had such rich pasturage that if the cattle were not checked they ate till they burst!

But about a century later, the Egyptian geographer, Ptolemy, produced a map of the world on which he shows the Mizzen Head, Cork Harbour, the River Shannon etc., and no doubt he obtained his information from sailors returned from Irish waters.

As regards the Romans, Agricola, the Roman Governor of Britain, about 80 A.D., met the first exiled malcontent Irishman, a petty chief, and contemplated invading Ireland, but did not do so, though the Romans may have raided our country, as Roman coins and statuettes have been found there, and it is locally stated in Cape Clear that there is a stone on the Island inscribed with Roman characters. However, there is no trace of recorded mercantile communication between Ireland and the Romans in the First Century A.D., though such commerce started soon after.

As time went on, the knowledge of Ireland, and its wealth, became common on the Continent which, no doubt, attracted the cupidity of the Danes and Norwegians (collectively known as the Danes), as they arrived in Ireland a few centuries later as we shall relate in the next chapter.

CHAPTER II

THE DANES

It is recorded that these Norsemen pillaged the Monastery on the Skelligs in 812 A.D., and ravaged Cape Clear later in 820, 824, 825 and 960, and Rosscarbery in 836, but these attacks seem to have been only raids and did not produce any permanent settlements in Carbery, unlike those at Dublin, Cork and Waterford.

We know now that the so-called "Danish forts", which were the homesteads of the early Irish, were not built or inhabited by the Danes, and it is thought that the local name arose owing to confusion between the word "Danaans" and Danes. On Horse Island, near Ballydehob, there is a deep vertical mine shaft which local tradition says was worked by the Danes, but this may mean that it is very ancient, as it is hard to believe that the raiders stayed long enough to undertake such a big job.

It is not easy to understand why the Danes should have troubled Cape Clear at all, as there does not seem to have ever been any monastery there with stores of gold and silver to attract them, so perhaps they only landed to take food and water? While, no doubt, these Norsemen looted all they could lay hands on, a modern writer suggests that they were ably assisted by local people who acted as guides and shared in the booty. It is of interest to mention that the celebrated Book of Kells, which disappeared in 1006 A.D., was found some months later minus its gold case, which shows the robbers valued the case more than the book.

These raids seem to have produced the round towers about which there were so many conjectures, and so much mystery, not many years ago, but which, it is now agreed, were erected from the 9th to the 12th century, A.D. as belfries to churches, for use as safe deposits when danger threatened.

There is a large fort at Lissacoha, near Schull, called "the fort of the battle", where a bloody fight is said to have taken place between the Irish and the Danes in which the latter were defeated.

We are told in our Irish History books that the power of the Danes was broken by Brian Boru at the celebrated Battle of Clontarf in 1014, but this battle certainly did not eradicate them as many of their settlements continued for long afterwards. In fact, we might consider the question whether this battle was not a mistake as, later on, when the Normans invaded Ireland, the Danes manfully but unsuccessfully resisted them, and, perhaps, if their power had not been broken at Clontarf, they might have united with the Irish and defeated the Normans, and so the history of Ireland might have been entirely altered?

All the Munster chiefs served at Clontarf and Cian (O'Mahony) a remarkably handsome man, whose stronghold was at Garranes, near Bandon, was in command of the South Munster men. They formed the Second Division of the Irish army, in the centre, and were opposed to the men of Leinster. Cian's kinsman, Donal, (ancestor of the O'Donoghues of Kerry) fought by his side, but on their march homewards they fell out and fought a battle between themselves in which Cian was killed, and the next year Donal was killed by Cian's son, Mahon, (from whom comes the tribal surname), so the O'Donoghues then packed up and moved into Kerry. It was at that time that Kinneigh Church and Round Tower were being built by the O'Mahonys.

It is of interest to mention that Cian's father was killed by Brian Boru, who then married his daughter, Sabia, to Cian, and from him comes the place name Enniskean, while from his grandfather, Bron, we get the name of Rossbrin. It is also of interest to state that Cian's fort at Garranes was recently excavated and yielded many objects of archaeological interest and that near it are the forts of his harper, trumpeter, poets, etc. St. Finbarr was born there, his father Amergin having been chief metal worker to the then ruling chief.

Another O'Mahony chief lived in a large fort at Ratherinane, near Ballydehob, which has a massive stone wall built to strengthen the earth rampart.

It is said of the Danes, and later of the dispossessed Irish clans, that they kept maps and records of their lost Irish lands, which they specifically passed on to their descendants by Deeds and Wills, hoping some time to recover them.

Some other items of local information which may be stated here are that in 684 A.D. the frost was so severe that the sea between Scotland and Ireland was frozen over enabling people to cross on the ice, and in 830 A.D. there was a great thunder storm and the sea broke Innisfadda (Long Island) into 3 parts now known as Long Island, Castle Island and Horse Island.

About the latter end of the 6th century, on Crab Fish Hill, on the Little Island (Inishbeg), Conall, Chieftain of Corca Laidhe, presented the Book of Dues to St. Fachtnan, the first Bishop of Rosscarbery, and, finally, we are told in the Annals of Innisfallen that, in 1104 A.D., "the son of O'hEidirsceoil, with 25 others, went out to sea and was never heard of again". What a splendid subject for an imaginative and romantic novel!

CHAPTER III

THE ANGLO-NORMAN INVASION

We have now come to the most important chapter in Irish History, as this invasion caused the most profound changes in the lives, language and laws of the people.

Before setting forth the local facts let us consider what led up to the invasion. Though the Irish people were then nominally Christians, there must have been much backsliding, because St. Malachi, Bishop of Connor, and later of Armagh, who died in 1148, described his flock as being Christian in name but pagan in fact, and he gave such a bad account of the Irish to St. Bernard in Rome that the latter stated he was surprised so saintly and loveable a man as Malachi could come come from such a barbarous race. The sins of the Irish which were complained of were survival of pagan or early Christian customs, uncanonical marriages, illegitimacy amongst the clergy and no giving of tithes or first fruits. It seems highly probable that these bad reports had much to say to the issuing of the famous Bull *"Laudabilliter"* in 1154 to Henry II, King of England, by Pope Adrian IV, who was the only Englishman ever made a pope, and who later was accused by the Irish chiefs of being prejudiced in favour of his own race. This Bull says:— "Henry has announced to us his desire to enter Ireland in order to subdue the people, to make them obedient to laws, and root out from among them the seeds of sin; the Irish are to accept him and obey him as their liege lord, and he shall enforce Peter's pence, and preserve the rights of the Church".

In 1172, Pope Alexander III, by letters, renewed Pope Adrian's grant. One of these, to the bishops, speaks of the foul customs of the Irish as made known to Rome by Letters Patent of the bishops themselves. They were directed to assist Henry in keeping possession of Ireland, and to censure those who should break their oaths of loyalty to him. A second Papal Letter directed Henry to continue his good work, while a third letter to the Kings and Princes of Ireland commended them for receiving Henry as King of their own free will. The lordship of Ireland was conferred by the Pope on Henry in vassalage to the Holy See.

Having thus obtained the blessing of the Church, Henry waited for a suitable pretext to commence operations, and, as so often happened in history, this pretext was supplied by a woman, and it is interesting to note that England, the most successful aggressor nation in history, committed her first act of aggression (or expansion as she would prefer to call it) in Ireland.

It seems strange that the Irish should have put up such a weak defence to the small army of invaders who came first, which did not exceed 2,000 men, including about 100 mail clad knights and men-at-arms. Even when Strongbow came in 1170 his force was only about double the first army. While we might class a mail-clad knight, mounted on a mail-clad horse, as a primitive form of tank, and new and terrifying to the Irish, still one would think that they could have collected a sufficient force of their lightly armed troups which, by mere weight of numbers, could sweep the small English armies into the sea. But the reverse is what happened, and in a short time the Irish accepted Henry as their King, and swore fealty to him, and Dermot McCarthy, King of Cork, was the first Irish King to do so.

Two possible reasons for this Irish collapse are suggested viz:—

First, that the Church was not against the invasion, and this weakened the fighting spirit of the chiefs. In fact, in 1170, the heads of the Irish Church decided the invasion was Divine vengeance for having purchased English slaves in Bristol, the great mart for this unholy trade, and the Bishops recommended that all such slaves still in bondage should be restored to freedom.

Secondly, that the Irish chiefs, who were fighting among themselves, thought that by accepting Henry they would secure him as an ally against their rivals. But, if this be true, they soon found their mistake, as Henry handed out huge estates to his Barons to keep them in hand as he himself had little authority over them, and they were semi-independent, and captured what they could. Arising out of these early grants, the Earls of Desmond who were FitzGeralds and Anglo-Normans, claimed to be chief overlords of all Cork and Kerry, a claim which they found it easier to state than to enforce, and, though McCarthy Mor and McCarthy Reagh admitted their claim, and agreed to pay tribute, it is doubtful if the Earls ever got much, if anything, from them.

In an old book we get the following rhyme which summarises the situation about the invasion very neatly:—

The Irish had long made the deuce of a clatter
And wrangled and fought about meum and tuum
Till England stept in and decided the matter
By kindly converting it all into suum.

To protect themselves from the Irish, the Normans built strongholds. At first these consisted of the mote and bailey type. The mote was an artificial circular earthen mound, about 30 feet high above its surrounding rampart, and it had a flat top, with a diameter of about 60 feet, on which were erected wooden buildings for the officers' quarters. On the ground level was another circular enclosure, of about 100 feet in diameter, also surrounded by a rampart, in which the soldiers were quartered. Both ramparts were palisaded with timber. Sometimes these strongholds were built on old Irish *duns* most of which were then unoccupied. There seem to be none of these primitive fortresses in our district, which suggests that the Normans did not come permanently into West Carbery till after 1200, when they were building the stone castles which are familiar to us. All these castles are Norman, or post-Norman, as, today, there is not in Ireland a trace of a pre-Norman castle, which it is believed were all made of wood and so have perished.

About 1215 the Normans built castles along the coast from Kenmare to Cork, including those at Kilcrohane, Donemark, Glandore, Baltimore and Donegal on Ringarogy Island. But many of the other castles still standing belong to a later period, and were built by Irish chieftains, and we shall deal with all these castles in a later chapter.

The coast line mentioned above, guarded by these Norman castles, was held by Barrys, Carews, Roches, de Courceys, Barrets, de Cogans (now Goggin), Arundells, Hodnetts, and others.

The invaders were not long left in peaceful occupation of Ireland for in 1173 we find McCarthy, King of Cork, unsuccessfully fighting against them. But better fortune was coming to the Irish, as, in 1261, Finghin McCarthy heavily defeated the Anglo-Normans at Callan Glen, near Kenmare, and the Carbery Irish followed up this success by recapturing most of the Norman castles in Carbery. It was in this way that McCarthy Reagh became possessed of Kilbrittain Castle (built by de Courcey), and the O'Donovans got Glandore Castle, and the O'Driscolls obtained the original castles at Dunasead (Baltimore) and Donegal (Ringarogy) which were built by Lord Slyine, or Sleviny, and which were later destroyed as we shall relate in another chapter.

A few months after Callan, Finghin was killed at Kinsale Harbour by de Courcey and de Cogan, and in return McCarthy Reagh, in 1291, killed de Courcey's grandson at Inchydowney. Finghin was the son of Donal Gott McCarthy who claimed descent from McCarthy, King of Cork. This branch dropped the title of King during the reign of Richard II, to whom, in 1395, Tadhg, the last King, made submission in very abject terms, and was afterwards known as McCarthy Mor.

Next to nothing is known of the history of Carbery for

nearly two centuries after the battle of Callan, but the Irish seem to have been mainly in control, for, about 1400, we find the subjects of Cork, Kinsale and Youghal petitioning Lord Rutland for military help, otherwise Munster would be lost. The document gives the yearly revenues of several English lords, including "Marquis of Caro", (whose descendant, Sir George Carew, we shall meet with later on), £2200 from "Dorzeyhaven" and other creeks, Lord Barnewale £1600 from Bearhaven and other creeks, and Lord Slynie £800 from Baltimore and havens and creeks. The document goes on to say that the power of these English lords was at one time equal to their property, that they had succeeded in hunting down the Irish and driving them like a pack of hungry wolves into a valley called Glenchought (in Kerry) between two great mountains, where they fed on "white meat" (probably rabbits), but that then the whole country was subject to them.

It was the first Marquis Carew who built Donemark Castle, near Bantry. He also seized Innisfadda (Long Island), and a townland "Colloghe-Chraige" (possibly Colla) by Schull Harbour. These two he gave as a present to his daughter on her marriage to the chief of the O'Mahonys. He also gave "the County of Moynterbarry", which is in the Parish of Kilcrohane, to the O'Dalys, who were bards, "to be his rimers or chroniclers". The Ordnance Map shows a great enclosure styled "O'Dalys Bardic School". Nearby they had a castle, but they paid no chief rent to McCarthy Reagh, and were subject to the O'Mahonys.

CHAPTER IV

SOME EFFECTS OF THE INVASION

When, or why, the name of Corca Laidhe became obsolete and Carbery came into common use in uncertain. Some say that the name Carbery came from a chief named Cairbre (Riada) who lived at the end of the 2nd Century A.D., or else from Cairbre, King of Munster, who flourished about 571 A.D. Others claim that Carbery was a tribal name of the O'Donovans who introduced it on their arrival about the time of the Norman invasion. Furthermore, it is well to mention that there are other Baronies of Carbery in the Counties of Kildare and Sligo with which of course we are not concerned.

The Normans introduced the feudal system into England, and then into Ireland. Under that system freehold land, on the death of the owner intestate, passed to the eldest son to the exclusion of the other children, based on the assumption that according to the custom prevalent in France, the eldest son was not the son of his reputed father but of the father's overlord. It seems curious that such a system, based on such an immoral custom and presumption, should still be allowed to prevail in this country as regards all fee simple property which is not registered in the Land Registry. This method of descent of land has been abolished in England and is manifestly unjust to the younger children. Under the same code all land was deemed to belong to the King who let it to his Earls or Counts, who sublet to Barons, who again sublet to commoners.

Arising out of this we get the word County as representing the estate of a Count, and County Cork was founded by King John in 1210 A.D. Similarly, the word Barony means the estate of a Baron and was supposed to contain 360 ploughlands. A ploughland was supposed to be the amount of land a single plough could break up in a year

15

and, normally, comprised 120 acres of arable land, with some rough pasture added, while an acre was supposed to be the area of ground a man could plough in a day with a pair of yokes. An Irish acre is considerably larger than an English one. From this are we to assume that an Irishman is a better ploughman than an Englishman? Is it not more likely that the English settlers shoved in a bit of extra Irish land into their acres, payment therefor being so much per acre?

The Civil Parish was also introduced, and often corresponds with the Irish division of Tuath, being the area of a sept or clan having its own chief, and is normally about one fourth of a Barony.

The original Barony of Carbery in County Cork was the largest Barony in Ireland. Over two centuries ago it was divided into East Carbery and West Carbery, the boundary being the stream running from Ballinlough Lake, through the ravine at Leap, into the sea. Under an Act passed in 1836, each of these two parts became subdivided by the Cork Grand Jury into two further divisions, East and West. Accordingly, we now have West Carbery (East Division), which includes Skibbereen, and West Carbery (West Division), which includes Kilcoe, and runs westward to the Mizzen and Kilcrohane. The boundary between these two divisions is a curious one. For example, Bauravilla and Bunalun are in West Division, while Cape Clear and Lisheen, which are geographically much farther West, are included in East Division. It is true that in some legal documents executed at the beginning of the 19th Century the Divisions are mentioned so perhaps the boundary followed some early tribal partition.

Changes have taken place, even in recent years, in the boundaries of ploughlands, or townlands to give them their modern name, and probably there also occurred amalgamations and subdivisions in olden times, otherwise it is hard to understand why the largest townland in Ireland, which is in County Mayo, should contain 7012 acres, while the smallest, which is in County Antrim, contains only 1¼ acres. Legal documents of a century ago call them "the town and lands", later shortened to townland, but it is difficult to believe that it was ever intended to build, or that there ever existed, a town on every ploughland. Another ancient measure of land was the gueeve which was 1/12th of a ploughland. This measurement continued in use up to about a century ago, and we still have a townland called "Gueeves" in the Parish of Aughadown.

The Irish system of land tenure and descent was very different from the English. While the Irish Chief had certain portions which he farmed as demesne lands by his tenants at will, and had also land which he conquered, or in which the ruling chief had disappeared, all of which he could dispose of amongst his relatives, over the bulk of tribe land he had only the following rights for life, and on his death they passed to the Tanist, his elected presumptive successor:—

1.   "Rising out" i.e. the subject clans were bound to assist him in war with all their forces.

2.   The right of being entertained with his personal followers at the expense of his subjects for a specified number of days at fixed periods of the year. Instead, he might require provisions, such as meat, honey, flour, brandy, ale, etc., to be sent to his house, or, instead, a money payment.

3.   A tribute from his vassal tribes in the nature of a land tax. His wife also got a tribute called "Lady's Gold". "Marriage cows" were also collected whenever the Chief's daughter married. Rents were usually calculated and paid in cows, and even fractions of cows, which were the normal currency. In 1161 a cow was worth 3 oz. of silver, but some centuries later was worth 6/8, being the equivalent of the well known advice fee payable to a lawyer! It was the Scandinavian Kings of Dublin who there introduced coined

money into Ireland, as up to then payments in cash were made by weight of gold or silver. A national coinage of Ireland was not issued until 1207, when King John minted same with a rude symbol of a harp on it.

4.   The right to quarter a certain number of soldiers, and in time of war to quarter all forces, on the farmers.

5.   Food for horses, dogs and huntsmen, when hunting, also hawks for hunting.

6.   Wages and victuals for workmen when constructing any work, or building a ship.

The chiefs of clans had similar rights over their own clans, and the petty chiefs of septs over their subjects, so, eventually the whole burden fell on the actual occupiers and tillers of the soil who consisted of freeholders or lesser gentry, the tenants at will, and last, but not least, the labourers some of whom were virtually slaves.

The Norman invaders, or the English as we can now call them, looked with disfavour on the Irish system, and Henry VIII, who reigned from 1509 to 1547, in opposition to his Dublin counsellors, who recommended the extermination of the native Irish, proposed to put the two races on an equality in law, to confiscate the large estates of absentee landowners, and to give the Irish chiefs Crown Grants of their land under English law, in exchange for a surrender of their titles according to Irish law, which would thus make their estates their absolute property, with hereditary succession, and so abolish the Tanists. The Irish chiefs were delighted with this plan as it gave them the absolute ownership of far more land than they had before, and they cheered Henry when he took the title of King of Ireland in 1541, but he died before his plan was completed, and it was his daughter, Queen Elizabeth, who finally introduced the "Policy of Grant and Regrant" as it was called.

Hitherto the septs had collective ownership of their land, (a primitive form of communism), and they were now overlooked, and personal grants in fee were made instead to the more powerful landowners, and so the small freeholders got squeezed out and became mere tenants at will to the chiefs, and it is claimed that this sowed the seed of all the later land agitation in Ireland.

In these Regrants, Quit Rents were reserved to the Crown, generally of 10/- per 120 acres, and these rents have been collected ever since by the State, though most of them have recently been redeemed under the various Land Purchase Acts.

The rights already mentioned of the lords and chiefs were also brought to an end by being compounded into Chief Rents, payable in cash, which have been paid also up to recently when most of them have been redeemed under the said Acts.

The clergy collected tithes of 1/10th of the produce of the land. After the suppression of the monasteries by Henry VIII, about 1542, the tithes they previously collected passed into lay hands and were called Impropriate Tithes. The Ecclesiastical Tithes were collected by the Church of Ireland up to the disestablishment of that Church in 1869 when, by Statute, they were transferred to the State. Most of these tithes, both Impropriate and Ecclesiastical, have been recently redeemed under the said Acts.

The chiefs of the four great tribes of West Carbery accepted Regrants, O'Driscoll in 1585, O'Mahony, O'Donovan and one of the McCarthys, in 1592, and McCarthy Reagh in 1596, while two of them were knighted, namely, Sir Owen McCarthy Reagh and Sir Fineen O'Driscoll.

In Carbery, prior to the rebellion of 1641, there were over 400 native land owners. Some of these, especially amongst the O'Driscolls and O'Donovans, had very minute portions of land, not always lying in one compact piece, but intermixed with other small fragmentary properties. It seems that no grants were made to the smaller land owners of

Carbery, so it is unknown how or when the individual clansmen were settled in their possessions, but they were looked on as the real owners of the clanlands and the old communal clan system of ownership disappeared.

CHAPTER V

THE 13TH TO THE 16TH CENTURIES

Relations between the English and the Irish were rapidly improving and the English were adopting the language and customs of the Irish to such an extent that it was said the English were becoming more Irish than the Irish themselves. In Curtis's "History of Mediaeval Ireland" it is stated:— "Intermarriages between Normans and Irish were more common in Munster than elsewhere, and the greater civilization and charm of its people already softened the relations of the two races"! And these intermarriages went on notwithstanding a very drastic Statute passed in 1367 which provided that if an Englishman should marry an Irish girl, or had her as his mistress, he was to be half hanged, then to be shamefully mutliated, and finally to be disembowelled when still alive, after which his estate was to be forfeited.

On the other hand, the Irish were learning much from the invaders, and began to build stone castles, and wear armour, and they brought gallowglasses (heavily armed professional soldiers) from the Hebrides (Scotland) into the North of Ireland, from whence they later came to Munster. These soldiers proved a great addition in battle to the lightly armed Irish kerne. It was in this way that the McDonnells, McSweeneys and McSheedys came into this country from Scotland. The Government was also trying to improve conditions and established Sheriffs, with juries to try criminal cases, and transferred the trial of cases relating to freeholds to the Crown Courts from the Lords Courts which were probably biassed. Other reliefs were also given. For instance, up to 1253 when the rule was abolished, when an Englishman lost anything, and got 6 other English people to swear an Irishman had taken it, the latter, though of good name and guiltless and backed by 30 or more witnesses, had to make restitution. But, unfortunately, the difference between the

21

two races was maintained, and, in 1300, a man who killed an Englishman was liable to a fine of 20 marks, but only to 5¼ marks for killing an Irishman, a mark being equivalent to 13s.4d. as a measure of money though never actually issued as a current coin.

In 1317 the Irish chiefs wrote a Remonstrance to the Avignon Pope, John XVII, against the treatment of Ireland by England. They pointed out that Pope Adrian "on false representation and blinded by English prejudice" had handed Ireland to Henry II. The chiefs complained of many things, including the fact that Irishmen were forbidden to be received into monasteries on English lands, and that lay and clerics asserted it was no more sin to kill an Irishman than a dog, and that an Irishman could not sue an Englishman. Some of these grievances were remedied a few years later when Irishmen were given the same right to life and limb as the English, and there was to be but one law for both English and Irish, except the 'unfree' or lowest class of labourers who remained virtually slaves until they were emancipated in 1605.

In 1338, from 2nd December until 10th February, there was such frost and snow that the Liffey was frozen hard and the people played, danced, and dressed their food, on the ice.

In 1368 we find the O'Driscolls of Baltimore joining the Norman Poers (known as the Poerini) in a raid on Waterford. They routed the City Army, slew the Mayor, Sheriff, 36 burghers, and 60 strangers trading in Waterford, and no doubt brought back much booty, as several sea expeditions by the O'Driscolls against Waterford followed. Waterford got some of its own back in 1413 when, on Christmas Day at suppertime, the Mayor and his men got into Baltimore Castle, and took as prisoners to Waterford O'Driscoll, and some of his relatives, and the Prior of some Abbey (but not Sherkin Abbey which was not then built). The Waterford men got into the Castle under the pretext that they were off a wine ship in the harbour and they enjoyed a dance and a carol with the usual drinking before they treacherously seized their prisoners. These raids became so prevalent that in 1450 a Statute was passed enacting that "as divers of the King's subjects has been slain by Fineen O'Hedriscoll, Chieftain of the Nation, no person of the Ports of Waterford, Wexford, etc. shall go within the country of the said O'Hedriscoll under heavy penalties of forfeitures etc." But still the raids went on, and in 1461 the Waterford men defeated the O'Driscolls and the Poers at Tramore.

The O'Driscolls overreached themselves in 1537 when four wine ships from Lisbon, en route for Waterford, were, on 20th February, driven by bad weather to Cape Clear, Baltimore and the Old Head of Kinsale. One of the ships, the "Santa Maria de Soci", seems to have run into Horshoe Bay, Sherkin Island, where she was boarded by Fineen O'Driscoll, Chieftain of Sherkin, and his sons, who offered to pilot her into Baltimore in return for 3 pipes of wine. We are told that it was Black Gilly O'Driscoll who did the piloting. The wine was so good the O'Driscolls fell from grace and, having invited the merchants and officers on the ship to a party in their castle, they were taken prisoners, and the O'Driscolls seized the wine and a right royal carouse followed.

This was too much for the Waterford men and they decided that, Statute or no Statute, the time had come for reprisals, so early in March they arrived in Baltimore with a small fleet and recaptured the ship, released the prisoners, and returned with the vessel to Waterford, but three fourths of the cargo was gone. Waterford was not yet satisfied and a larger fleet, consisting of the great galley and two other ships, with 400 men on board, arrived in Baltimore Harbour at the end of March, anchored off Dunalong Castle, and besieged and captured it, and tumbled some of its outworks into the sea. They then wrecked Sherkin Abbey, called Friars Minor, and a large mill adjoining it, and went through Reengarogy and 'Inchepite' (probably Spanish Island) with fire and sword. On Inchepite we are told Fineen had "his most pleasant seat in a castle, adjoining to a hall, with an orchard and green, all of which were destroyed and razed to the earth". The Down Survey shows Spanish Island otherwise Inispicke. The Waterford men wound up by burning Baltimore, and breaking down Teighe O'Driscoll's goodly castle and baun (presumably Dunasead). They also captured and took away Fineen's great galley and 40 pinnaces, and sank another 40 pinnaces, and then "returned on Good Friday with great joy and comfort". It is thought that Fineen and Teighe were brothers.

We are told that Black Gilly fought to a finish in one of the castles and finally blew it up with attackers and attacked in it; also that one of the Waterford men named Grant escaped from the top of a burning castle, by having an arrow shot to him with a cord attached, which he made fast to the building and down which he slid.

If, indeed, the old castle of Dunasead was destroyed, then the present ruin in Baltimore cannot have been built sooner than the middle of the 16th century, and it certainly looks more like an Elizabethan fortified house than a Norman Castle. This is corroborated by Carew who, writing about it in 1602, calls it a "house" while he calls Dunalong a "castle".

This sharp lesson by the Waterford men seems to have had an effect on the O'Driscolls for, on 13th December, 1551, there is on record a Pardon to "McCon M'Fineen Driscoll of Ballitimore", and other Driscolls, for the deaths of "Dunevan McDonnell McDermot and Driscoll and their companions being pirates".

It appears O'Driscoll executed 11 men (including 3 of his own clansmen) for piracy and then obtained a pardon as above for his drastic action.

But piracy was not confined to the O'Driscolls, for

Donal O'Mahony of Rossbrin was seized in Cork in 1562, tried on a charge of piracy, and executed. Furthermore, he was attainted, and his castle and lands of Rossbrin were forfeited. Canon O'Mahony suggests that the piracy complained of consisted of chasing as far as Cork a British ship which was preventing foreign ships from entering O'Mahony harbours. Rossbrin Castle was then handed over to other O'Mahonys, but in 1571 the authorities again took possession, and put McSweeney gallowglasses in charge on behalf of the Queen, but they became too friendly with the O'Mahonys so were removed, and the castle was let to a brother of Donal at a small rent.

About 1496 a bard of Rossbrin Castle wrote a poem, known as *The Psalter of Rossbrin*, about the O'Mahonys which, unfortunately, is lost, as is also *The Book of Timoleague.*

A final item of local interest during this period is that, in August 1488, Pope Innocent VIII issued a Bull of Excommunication against Bishop Thaddeus McCarthy, styled therein "son of iniquity", because he grabbed the See of Ross from Bishop Odo. However, Thaddeus made his peace later and was reinstated as Bishop, and, in 1490, he was transferred to the See of Cork and Cloyne, and he died about 2 years later.

CHAPTER VI

THE DESMOND REBELLION AND AFTER

It is not part of our story to give details of this long protracted rebellion by the Desmonds who, though Anglo Normans, had become Irish in their sympathies. It commenced in 1567 and continued intermittently till 1583 when the Earl of Desmond was killed. The fighting during this long period made Munster into a desert. The poet Spenser, who lived at Kilcoleman, near Mallow, writing in 1596, gives the following account of Munster at that time "notwithstanding that the same was a most rich and plentiful country, full of corn and cattle, that you would have thought that they should have been able to stand long, yet ere one year and a half they were brought to such wretchedness as that any stony heart would have rued the same. Out of every corner of the woods and glens they came, creeping forth upon their hands, for their legs could not bear them, they looked like anatomies of death, they spoke like ghosts crying out of their graves, they did eat the dead carrions, happy where they could find them, yea, and one another soon after, insomuch as the very carcases they spared not to scrape out of their graves, and if they found a plot of water-cresses or shamrocks there they flocked as to a feast for the time, yet not able long to continue there withal, that in short space there were none almost left, and a most populous and plentiful country suddenly left void of men and beast, yet sure in all that war there perished not many by the sword, but all by the extremity of famine which they themselves had wrought". It looks as if the West Carbery chiefs as a whole did not join in the rising. Perhaps the reason for this was that in 1521 the Earl of Desmond attacked the McCarthys of Muskerry, who were joined by McCarthy Reagh, the O'Mahonys and other Carbery chiefs and the allies inflicted a severe defeat on the Earl at Mourne Abbey, and he only saved himself by flight. Besides, the Earl, as previously mentioned, claimed to be overlord of all Carbery, and entitled to tribute thereout, which probably did not add to his popularity with the West Carbery chiefs, though McCarthy Mor was glad to accept a grant of the Earl's claim on the forfeiture of his estate after the rebellion.

However, in case of accidents, Sir William Pelham, the Lord Justice, took Sir Owen McCarthy Reagh and 15 other chiefs and gentlemen to Limerick to keep them out of harm's way, but Sir Owen's brother Donogh, actively assisted the English.

Donald McCarthy was attainted in 1573, for murdering his kinsman McCarthy of Kilcoe, and his castle and lands at Cloghane and Lissangle were confiscated, but 4 years later they were given back to another McCarthy who sold same to Sir Walter Coppinger as we shall see later.

There is on record a general pardon granted in 1583 to Fineen O'Driscoll and others so they must also have been implicated to some extent in the rebellion.

O'Mahony of Rossbrin was also attainted and his castle and demesne of 1080 acres were confiscated and leased to Oliver Lambert in 1584, who surrendered his Lease in 1602, and the property was then leased to Morgan and finally passed away from the O'Mahonys. In 1852, we find the Manor of Rossbrin owned by George, Lord Baron Audley, as in that year his estate was sold by the Incumbered Estates Court. Later, the Edinburgh Life Assurance Co. acquired the property, and sold it to the tenants under the Land Acts.

O'Mahony of Dunbeacon also got into trouble, and his castle being confiscated was burned by him, and the property passed into the ownership of Sir William Hull who will appear again in our story.

Conogher O'Mahony of Kinalmeaky (Bandon) also joined the Earl of Desmond, and shared his fate as he was killed in 1582, and his estate of 36,000 acres was confiscated, and one third of it was granted to Fane Becher, the founder of the Becher family in West Carbery, on condition that he planted 86 English Protestant families on this estate and paid a Quit Rend of £66.13.4. Becher landed in Kinsale in 1586, and his Patent is dated 30th September, 1588, and soon after he and his followers founded the town of Bandon. He brought over a number of English settlers and others soon followed, and many of their names are still well known locally, such as Atkins, Alcock, Bernard, Baldwin, Biggs, Bennett, Brookes, Beamish, Carey, Cox, Daunt, Emerson, Fleming, Fuller, Hoskins, Kent, Kingston, Lane, Lambert, Mansfield, Poole, Russell, Stanley, Seymour, Shorten, Skuce, Teape, Trinder, Travers, Varian, Welply and Wolfe.

Becher seems to have acted very considerately as he did not disturb the Irish tenants, and he even offered the then O'Mahony (Donal) to divide the estate with him, but this was refused, and Donal attacked Becher and burned Castle Mahon (Bandon) and continued to give trouble till his death in 1594.

In 1598, owing to O'Neill's rebellion, Becher fled from Castle Mahon and Dermod (brother of Conagher deceased) retook Kinalmeaky. He died in 1599 and was succeeded by his brother, Maolmuadh, who was the last chief of Kinalmeaky. After Becher's return, at the close of O'Neill's rebellion, he seems to have allowed Maolmuadh to occupy Killowen till his death and he was buried in Timoleague Abbey. His son probably went to Spain, and nothing is known of him, and so ended the O'Mahony chiefs of Kinalmeaky.

Becher himself did not long enjoy the property, and he was succeeded by his son, Henry, in 1595, who became Sir Henry, and Lord President of Munster, in 1604, and after his death (in 1610) the Kinalmeaky property was sold to the Great Earl of Cork save Castle Mahon which was sold to Francis Bernard. The Bechers then moved to West Carbery, and we shall have much to tell of them later on.

Soon after the Desmond rebellion a kind of Census of the forces and property of the great tribes of South Munster was made from which we get a fair idea of their comparative importance and of the location of their territories. In 1588 it is recorded that McCarthy Reagh had 60 horsemen, 80 gallowglasses, and 2000 kerne. The O'Mahonys of Ivagha had 72 horsemen and 220 kerne. O'Sullivan Beare had 10 horsemen and 200 kerne. The O'Driscolls of Baltimore had 6 horsemen and 200 kerne and O'Donovan had 6 horsemen and 60 kerne. Even added together they made only a small army and the figures are not impressive but, on the other hand, the whole population of Ireland in 1652 is stated to have been only 850,000 while 20 years later it had increased to 1,320,000. The fighting and desolation caused by the 3 big rebellions shortly before 1652, and the subsequent deportations, no doubt, account for the small population in 1652, while the subsequent increase in 1672 may be accounted for in part by the flood of settlers who came in in Cromwell's time.

As regards the territories, at the extreme West we find the O'Mahonys in possession of the Parishes of Kilmoe and Schull, with the islands off their coast, such as Castle Island and Long Island. They were fond of building castles and had 12 in all. The chief one was White Castle (Ardintenant), also Rossbrin, Dunlough (3 Castle Head), Black Castle on Castle Island, Leamcon, Ballydevlin, Lissagriffin, Castle Mehigan (the O'Mehigans being bards to the O'Mahonys), Dunmanus, Dunbeacon, Knockeens and Dunkelly. The O'Mahonys paid a chief rent of £30 to McCarthy Reagh.

Next came several branches of the McCarthys, the principal ones being Clan Dermod, Clan Teighe Roe and Clan Teighe Ilen. Clan Dermod had the Parish of Kilcoe, and the south part of Caheragh, and parts of Castlehaven and Kilmacabea, and the north part of Abbeystrowery Parish. They had 3 castles viz:--Kilcoe, Cloghan (now Lissangle) and

Ballyouiane.

Clan Teighe Roe had the Parish of Durrus, the north part of Caheragh, and part of Kilmacomogue (Bantry).

Clan Teighe Ilen had a small district of 27 ploughlands on both sides of the River Ilen, near Skibbereen, which included most of the Parish of Abbeystrowery and a few of the southern townlands of Caheragh Parish. But Skibbereen itself, with the detached part of the Parish of Creagh on which it stands, belonged to McCarthy Reagh as demesne lands, on which he had the two castles of Gortnaclohy and Lettertinlish, both of which have completely disappeared.

Then came the O'Driscolls who were in two sections, viz:—Collymore, ruled by O'Driscoll Mor, and Collybeg, ruled by O'Driscoll Oge.

The latter district was almost coterminous with the Parish of Aughadown and comprised the land between the Ilen at Newcourt, and Roaring Water Bay, and included 34 ploughlands, with Rincolisky Castle (Whitehall) and Hare Island and one of the Skeam Islands. This district paid a chief rent of £10.10.11. to McCarthy Reagh.

Collymore was larger, comprising the Parishes of Tullagh and Creagh, with the islands of Clear, Sherkin, Ringarogy and Inishbeg. The district had 39½ ploughlands on the mainland, and 25½ in the islands, with at least 7 castles thereon, viz:— Dunasead, Donalong, Donegal, Dunamore (Cape Clear), Ardagh, Oldcourt and Cloghan (Lough Hyne Island). In addition Collymore had a strip of the coast between Toe Head and Castlehaven containing 5½ ploughlands, with Castlehaven Castle, this district being known as Glenbaraghan. The mainland part of Collymore was bounded on the north and west by the River Ilen, and on the south by the sea. The eastern boundary seems to have roughly followed the Compass Hill Road from the river, over Coom Hill to Tragumna, and then up the hill beyond through the old road on to Toe Head.

Collymore paid a Chief Rent of £27.11.11½. to McCarthy Reagh, and in addition was liable to pay 8 cows, or 8 nobles, to the Earl of Desmond. Furthermore the Bishop of Ross was entitled to 20/- yearly out of 3 ploughlands of Tullagh and 36/- per year out of Sherkin. On the other hand O'Driscoll collected chief rents amounting to £18.5.11. from his under chiefs.

Last came the O'Donovans with 131 ploughlands, divided also into two sections, Clan Cahil with 67 ploughlands, and Clan Loughlin with 64. These two names belonged to the sons of Crom O'Donovan who was killed in 1254, near Enniskeane, in a fight with the O'Mahonys.

Clan Cahil had the Parishes of Drimoleague, Drinagh and Myross, with 3 castles, viz:—Raheen, Castle Donovan and Castle Ire (or Ivor).

Clan Loughlin had the Parish of Kilfaughnabeg, with large parts of Kilmacabea, Ross, Kilmeen, and parts of Castlehaven and Caheragh. This clan had Glandore and Kilfinnan Castles, and may also have had Benduff Castle, though possibly this belonged to McCarthy Reagh.

Clan Cahil collected dues from all havens from the head of Glandore Harbour westwards to Castlehaven, and Clan Loughlin eastwards to the Roury River.

As regards McCarthy Reagh, as overlord of Carbery he received Chief Rents totalling £208.14.1½. per year, besides a "poundage hog", or one hog out of every herd of 5 or upwards in certain districts, including Lurriga, and certain free ploughing and measures of wheat. As rents were normally paid in cows (3 to the £), this chief collected some 624 cows per year, and, in addition, he had 70½ ploughlands which he farmed at his demesne, so he was a very wealthy man.

At a McCarthy Reagh Inquisition, taken in 1636, it is recorded that he was entitled to a poundage hog out of Lurriga and some townlands running on to near Bantry. As hogs were then fed in woods we can assume that there were no woods then left nearer to the southern sea coast.

CHAPTER VII

THE REBELLION OF 1600 TO 1603

We now come to the rebellion of O'Neill and O'Donnell, which began in 1595, and was not finally terminated till 1603, about a year after the disastrous Battle of Kinsale.

We get a great deal of information about the happenings in West Carbery during the years 1600 to 1603 from the book known as *"Pacata Hibernia"*, meaning of course "Ireland pacified", which was surely a misnomer, seeing that the work was only published in 1633, while in 1641, 8 years later, there was another rebellion! The book was produced by Thomas Stafford, who seems to have been a Lieutenant, but whose only recorded exploit is that during the siege of Dunboy, when in company with Captain Gowen Harvey and some others, in 3 boats, they killed 8 unfortunate Irishmen who tried to escape by swimming. It is thought, however that the book was in fact written, or dictated, by Sir George Carew, Lord President of Munster, who was later made Earl of Totnes, but who was dead when it was published. Carew was a descendant of the Marquis Carew already mentioned, and he seems to have had an intense hatred of the Irish, probably because his brother had been killed at Glenmalure, Co. Wicklow, in the Desmond rebellion in 1580, and also his ancestor, the Marquis, had lost his estates between Bantry and Dursey Island some centuries before.

The dates in the book are confusing owing to the change in the Calendar, made shortly before in some countries, but not till later in England and Ireland. The change became necessary owing to the fact that in the Calendar issued by Julius Caesar, some 1600 years before, the exact length of the year was miscalculated and made too short, with the result that the calendar date was falling steadily behind the actual time. To remedy this, Pope Gregory XII instructed a German Jesuit, known as Clavius, to work out a new

33

Calendar, which he did in 1582, and put the matter right by inserting an extra day in Leap Years. The 10 days then in arrear were simply omitted so 4th October that year was followed by 15th October. Furthermore the old system of ending the calendar year on 24th March was altered to 31st December. In some countries the new Calendar was adopted at once, but Great Britain did not fall into line until 1752 when 11 days had to be omitted and 2nd September that year was followed by 14th September. Ireland followed suit in 1782, but Russia did not change her Calendar until 1902. It is said that the monks on the Skelligs refused to follow the new Calendar, hence marriages could be solemnized there at least 11 days after Lent had commenced on the mainland, which originated the Skellig Lists popular in our district up to recent years, which were issued by local wags at the beginning of Lent and in which named bachelors and spinsters were advised in doggerel rhyme to proceed to the Skelligs at once and get married before the arrears of time there should have expired and Lent should have started also in the Islands.

In the *Pacata Hibernia* the old Calendar is generally used, but sometimes the new date appears, and in such cases the words "stilo novo", or "new style", appear in the margin. Until one understands the old Calendar, it is startling to read in the *Pacata* of an event happening in December of one year followed by a later event occurring in January or February of the same Calendar year.

Carew received his appointment in March 1600 (new style) his yearly "wages" being only £133.6.8., with a guard of 30 horsemen and 20 footmen, and 2/- per day for his captain and trumpeter, and these were surely small wages, even for those days, considering that Carew was given power, amongst many other things, "to execute martial law", "to oppress any rebel with sword and fire", "to put a suspected party to torture", to inflict or remit the death penalty, and even to interfere in church matters and punish Bishops who were slack in their duties. But Carew was directed, if possible, not to execute martial law on any person having £5 of freehold, or goods value for £10, but to have them tried by the Common law. In other words, he was authorised to massacre the poor people out of hand, but the wealthier people only after trial. He carried out his instructions thoroughly by destroying growing crops, slaughtering live stock, burning and blowing up castles and houses, and killing all and sundry, including prisoners.

On his arrival all the West Carbery chiefs seem to have held themselves aloof from the rebellion until after the Spaniards arrived in 1601, and, indeed, O'Mahony and the O'Crowleys sought for and obtained protection from Sir Richard Percy at Kinsale, and the celebrated Florence McCarthy (McCarthy Mor) submitted on his knees to Carew, while Sir Owen McCarthy Reagh remained loyal to Queen Elizabeth throughout, and even joined her forces, but his 2 sons joined the rebels.

But Carew had no faith in either Florence McCarthy or Maolmuadh O'Mahony, the last chief of Kinalmeaky, and he arrested both of them in the summer of 1601.

Notwithstanding the peace existing in Carbery, Captain Flower and his men, operating under Carew, in April 1600 started from Rosscarbery, crossed "the Leap", and raided and burned O'Donovan's country for 3 days, and killed 500 cows they could not bring back with them.

Again, in September 1600, Sir R. Percy marched from Kinsale to Rosscarbery, guided by Walter Coppinger of Cork (who presumably was the same person as Sir Walter Coppinger, who later will figure largely in our story). The *Pacata* says they were disappointed of "doing service thereabout", so "marched beyond the Leape, and coming suddenly to Kilcoe, they took there a prey of 300 cows, which they brought in safety without any loss to Lettertinlis

(Skibbereen), and from thence they returned again to their garrison". And during December following Sir Richard Percy raided the O'Mahony country at Kinalmeaky, near Bandon, to commandeer some cattle, but was attacked and beaten off by O'Mahony and Florence McCarthy's brother, and the English failed to take any spoil, much to their chagrin.

Meantime the Irish were foolishly dissipating their strength in quarrels between themselves, in which they were encouraged by the English who then, as now, made a point of sowing dissension amongst their enemies. Here are two examples of these dissensions given in *Pacata Hibernia*. Cattle raids, with ensuing fights, seem to have been a national form of sport in Ireland for centuries, and so we are told that in 1600 McCarthy Reagh's followers, returning from a punitive expedition following a cattle raid, were attacked by the O'Learys, and, after a sharp fight, the chief of the O'Learys, and ten lesser chiefs of their clan, were killed. Again in 1602 we read that a cousin of McCarthy Reagh took the liberty of taking some of the latter's cattle, which was resisted, and in the ensuing fight the cousin was killed.

Carew investigated the causes leading up to the rebellion and found they were principally (1) Religion, (2) the undertakers (i.e. English settlers) encroaching upon gentlemen's lands, (3) fear for the safety of their lives, (4) the composition rent demanded by the Crown, and (5) extortions and unlawful acts of Sheriffs and other officials. On top of all this the Queen instituted a new coinage for Ireland by which 20/- English was made equivalent to 21/- Irish, but all the people in Ireland (both English and Irish) were so hostile to this new money that both Carew and the Deputy (or Viceroy) Lord Mountjoy had to write to England urging that it should be abolished.

It is of interest to mention that Carew considered that the towns were the principal upholders of the rebellion, on which they were getting rich, as he says the soldiers spent their money in the towns, and the merchants bought goods from the country cheaply, while they sold goods underhand (i.e. in the "black market") to the rebels at excessive prices, and he adds that the towns elected "lawless lawyers" to be their mayors and chief officers, presumably to protect them in their unlawful dealings. The towns at that time were very small and, from the Spaniards who landed in Kinsale in October 1601, we learn that town did not contain above 200 houses, so the population must have been under 2,000.

On their way to Kinsale some of the Spanish ships, with 700 soldiers on board, were driven into Baltimore, but, eventually, all got to Kinsale, the entire Spanish force numbering only about 3,400 men, with 4 cannon. They complained that only a few Irish joined them, who had no armour, and only small horses with saddles and no stirrups, and that they fought only with half pikes. The English then collected their forces, to the number of 12,000 with 6 cannon. Part of this force, consisting of 1,000 foot and 100 horse in 13 ships, under the command of O'Brien, Earl of Thomond, came from England, and they were driven by the weather to the westward and it was only with difficulty they got into Castlehaven, and they had to wait some days there before they could proceed to Kinsale.

Early in December 1601, 6 more Spanish ships arrived in Castlehaven with 700 soldiers and several cannon, which were disembarked there, and it was promised that further reinforcements were coming. This produced too great a strain on the lukewarm loyalty of the local chiefs and, almost to a man, they rose in rebellion. The most notable exception was Sir Owen McCarthy Reagh, but his sons joined the Spaniards, as did also Sir Fineen O'Driscoll and all the other O'Driscolls, and almost all the McCarthys, as well as the O'Mahonys, O'Donovans and O'Sullivans.

Donagh O'Driscoll delivered to the Spaniards his castle at Castlehaven, Sir Fineen (of whom the *Pacata Hibernia* says that "never in the course of his whole life had he been tainted with the least spot of disloyalty") gave them his castles at Dunasead (Baltimore) and Dunalong (Sherkin) and O'Sullivan gave them his castle at Dunboy (Castletown Berehaven). The Spaniards placed a garrison of 100 men and 8 cannon in Castlehaven, 50 men each in Dunasead and Dunalong with 2 cannon, and 100 men and 10 cannon in Dunboy. O'Donovan, and the two sons of McCarthy Reagh, each received 100 Spaniards to help them. The Spanish entrenchments, their ovens where it is said their cannon balls were cast, the site of their "general house" (probably Barracks) and some of their graves are still to be seen on Reen Point opposite the site of Castlehaven Castle. This building, which was for a long time in a damaged and shaky condition, collapsed entirely in 1926 and is now only a heap of rubble almost covered with wild flowers and weeds.

About a week after the landing of the Spaniards, Sir Richard Levison came from Kinsale, with 6 English warships, and attacked the Spanish fleet in Castlehaven Harbour. He claimed he sank one of their ships and drove 3 others ashore. He then tried to get out of the harbour, but, the wind being adverse, he was kept there for 24 hours, and received 300 shot through hull, mast and tackle from 5 cannon which the Spaniards had put ashore to defend the harbour. The weather having calmed, he got towed out by his boats and then sailed back to Kinsale. The Ordnance Map shows the site of a Battery on the point not far from the Castle, and opposite Reen point, which is probably where the Spanish guns were planted. The Irish account of this naval fight differs considerably, as O'Sullivan Bere claims that the English lost 575 men, while the Spaniards had only one man killed and one wounded, and the Irish had only one man wounded.

It is not part of our story to give details of the siege and battle of Kinsale. Suffice it to say that the Irish Army, under

O'Neill and O'Donnell, was completely routed on 3rd
January 1602 (new style) and the Spaniards a week later
agreed to surrender Kinsale, and the castles at Castlehaven,
Baltimore and Dunboy, and to return to Spain. Three points
of interest may however be mentioned, viz:—1st, that Red
Hugh O'Donnell, after the battle, sailed from Castlehaven to
Spain, where he died shortly after. The 2nd point is that the
Spanish speak of "disengaging" themselves, so that term, so
commonly used in World War No. 2 communiques, is over
300 years old. The 3rd point is that it was an Irish traitor
who warned the English of the proposed attack by the Irish,
and so destroyed their chances of a surprise. The *Pacata* gives
the traitor's name as Brien MacHugh Oge MacMahon and says
he was a principal commander in the Irish army. He first sent
to Carew for a bottle of "Aquavitae", otherwise brandy, and,
this being sent, he returned thanks, and gave the information
of the planned attack, so brandy proved the undoing of the
Irish and Spaniards. On 7th January, 1601 (old style), or
January 1602 (new style), Carew granted a Commission to
his friend and relative, Captain Roger Harvey, brother of
Captain Gawen Harvey, giving him authority from
Rosscarbery to the bounds of Beare and Bantry, to exercise
the same powers of life and death, fire and sword, and
martial law, as Carew himself possessed, save that the
execution of martial law was limited to freeholders under £2
instead of £5.

Captain Harvey entered with zest on his duties and
arrived at Castlehaven on 21st February 1602 (new style), to
find that the O'Driscolls had got back into their Castle and
the Spaniards were attacking and undermining it. On the
sight of the English ships the O'Driscolls departed, and the
Spaniards then surrendered the castle to Captain Harvey who
was entertained "with great humanity" by Pedro de Soto, the
Spanish leader. Gawen Harvey was left in charge of this
Castle with 100 men, while Roger and de Soto sailed on to

Baltimore and were feasted in Dunalong (Sherkin). On 7th March 1602 (new style) this Castle and Dunasead (Baltimore) were surrendered to Roger Harvey and the Spaniards set sail for Spain.

Meantime, Harvey sent a party of his men to Cape Clear, the Castle which was guarded by Captain Tyrell's Irishmen, and the English failed to capture it, but they pillaged the island and brought back 3 boats. Two days later the Irish garrison in Cape Clear left, and Harvey placed a guard in that Castle (Dunamore), and about the same time Sir Fineen O'Driscoll came to Captain Harvey and surrendered himself. While in Sherkin, Harvey and de Soto had a very interesting conversation which is given in detail in *Pacata Hibernia*. They discussed religion and high politics, and de Soto admitted that the Spaniards came to Ireland, not for religion or conscience, but only for revenge because the English opposed the Spaniards on the Continent. De Soto also alleged that the Irish were "a barbarous nation for which Christ never died"!

On 2nd April 1602 (new style), Mountjoy and Carew sent their report to England and it stated "As for Sir Fineen O'Driscoll, O'Donovan, and the two sons of Sir Owen McCarthy, they and their followers since their coming in are grown very odious to the rebels of those parts, and are so well divided in factions amongst themselves, as they are fallen to preying and killing one another, which we consider will much avail to the quieting of those parts", which gives a truly melancholy picture of Irish unity, or rather the lack of it, at that time. The report also gives the interesting information that the English soldiers received rations of 2 lbs. of beef on flesh days, and 8 herrings on fish days, and they nearly mutinied when it was suggested that those rations should be reduced by ½ lb. of beef or 2 herrings.

In mid March 1602 the Earl of Thomond, and with him 2500 foot and 50 horsemen, were sent by Carew to burn the rebels' corn in Carbery, Beare and Bantry, to take their cows, and commence hostilities against them. He was directed, however, to afford all kind and mild usage to those who were in subjection, or lately protected, as O'Driscoll, O'Donovan, and Sir Owen McCarthy's sons, and also to give all the comfort he might to Owen O'Sullivan. This man (Owen) though a cousin, was also an enemy of O'Sullivan Beare and he later took an active part in the capture of Dursey Island, and the massacre of its inhabitants who were his own countrymen, and in looting cattle for the English army, and he also captured and looted Dunmanus Castle. The Earl was also directed to take possession of Dunasead, Sir Fineen's "house", in which of necessity the store of victuals and munitions for the garrison of Baltimore should be laid, for the "castle" of Dunalong, where Roger Harvey was, was too small for that purpose. It will be noted that Dunasead is called a house and Dunalong a castle. The Earl went as far as Bantry, placed some garrisons, and then returned and joined Carew.

About this time there arrived in Castlehaven, from Spain, the Jesuit, Domenick Collins, in a cargo ship commanded by Jago. He slept two nights in Gortnaclohy Castle, (which stood on Castlelands, near Skibbereen, but has since completely disappeared), and then went on to Dunboy, where he was captured by Carew, and was hanged on 31st October, 1602, in Youghal, where also he was born.

Carew now prepared to march in person with his army to attack Dunboy, and he arrived in Rosscarbery on 4th May 1602 (new style). Next day he went "over the Leape" to Glenbarrahane and inspected Castlehaven Castle and harbour. The following day he, with his regiment, went to Baltimore, and he also visited Sherkin. Meantime, the Earl of Thomond and Sir Richard Percy went to Oldcourt Castle and stayed there 2 nights. The whole army then moved on, and encamped on a mountain at a place called "Recareneltaghe"

(possibly Reencorreen) near Kilcoe Castle, which was held by
Conogher O'Driscoll, (eldest son of Sir Fineen), who was still
in rebellion. Then the army went on to Donemark, near
Bantry, where there was a castle originally built by Carew's
ancestor, the Marquis Carew, some centuries before. It is
outside the scope of our story to follow this army of 4000
men to Castletownberehaven where, in June 1602, they
captured Dunboy Castle and to a man massacred the garrison
of 143, (including Florence O'Driscoll who was known as
Captain Cain), and did the same in Dursey Island. Captain
Roger Harvey was present at the siege of Dunboy and was
bruised, but not seriously wounded, by stones and iron
bullets flung on him, and he was one of those in the vault of
Dunboy when MacGeoghegan, the commander of the castle,
though mortally wounded, made a gallant but unsuccessful
effort to blow up both besiegers and besieged.

Just before the siege a Spanish ship arrived in
Kilmacillogue, near Berehaven, and landed Owen MacEgan,
who was Bishop of Ross and Apostolic Vicar, and some
others. They brought some thousands of pounds, and other
supplies, with them, and some of the money was distributed
and, amongst others, it is alleged that O'Donovan received
£200., the McCarthys £860., and the O'Driscolls, £500. This
money, and the exhortations of the Bishop, had the effect of
fanning the flames of rebellion, notwithstanding the dreadful
fate of the Dunboy garrison, and some who had submitted
again rose in rebellion. Eight days after Dunboy fell a party
of Roger Harvey's Company captured Leamcon Castle, and
two days later the army on its way to Cork came to the castle
of Lettertinlish, near Skibbereen (now disappeared), then
held by Conogher O'Driscoll with a garrison of 17 men.
After a short defence, and some shots discharged, the
garrison surrendered on their lives being spared and, after the
soldiers pillaged the goods, they burned and destroyed the
castle and stone hall, and then the army continued to

Rosscarbery.

Garrisons were then, in July 1602, stationed round the country. Captain Roger Harvey, and his brother Gawen, remained at Baltimore and Castlehaven respectively. Lord Barry's Company was at Lettertinlish, The Treasurer's Company was at "The Abbey of Strory", Captain Stafford was at Oldcourt, and Captain Slingsby was at the Church of "Shadone". The *Pacata Hibernia* boasts that these garrisons left "neither corn, nor horn, nor house, unburnt" between Ross and Bantry.

In addition to the Castles already mentioned the following were then captured by the English:—Donegal, the Downings and Rincolisky, and in fact all that stood by the seaside between Dunboy and Castlehaven, except Kilcoe and Cloghan. There are 2 castles called Cloghan, viz: the one on the Island in Lough Hyne which belonged to the O'Driscolls, and the other on Lissangle which belonged to Coppinger. As some, at least, of the O'Driscolls were still rebels, and as Coppinger was a loyal subject, it seems probable that it is the Lough Hyne Castle which is referred to in *Pacata Hibernia*.

Roger Harvey died before the end of 1602, and we are not told the place of his death or burial but, presumably, it was in Baltimore or Sherkin. We are told, however, that his surgeon reported that "his heart was blown like a bladder". He was succeeded in his command by Captain George Flower from Bantry, with whom we are already acquainted, whose first recorded act in this command was, in company with Captains Slingsby and Stafford, to attack Cloghan Castle, mainly because a priest had lately arrived there from Rome. Flower had with him as prisoner the brother of the constable of the castle, and he threatened the garrison that if they did not surrender he would hang his prisoner in their sight. To save the priest, the Constable refused to surrender and Flower hanged his prisoner as threatened. Four days later the garrison surrendered, but in the meantime they had got the priest away safely. The last castle to fall was Kilcoe, which Flower took in February 1603. It is described as a place of great strength and the only castle in Carbery that held out in rebellion.

The fighting in Carbery ended early in 1602 in a skirmish at "Cladach", or "Grillagh", west of Ballineen, in which the sons of Sir Owen McCarthy, a brother of Florence McCarthy, Dermod O'Driscoll and Teighe O'Mahony took part. Seeing the fighting going against them, Bishop MacEgan, at the head of 100 men, and with his drawn sword in one hand and his beads in the other, charged the English. In the fight which followed the Bishop was shot dead, and his followers lost heart and ran, and even threw themselves into the Bandon River, but we are told by Carew that most of them were killed or drowned. After this the McCarthys asked for pardon and received it, but Teighe O'Mahony, brother of the chief of Kinalmeaky was captured and beheaded, and the Bishop's chaplain was also executed. The Bishop's papers were seized, and amongst them was an Indulgence dated 18th April 1600, from Pope Clement VIII, granting full remission of sins to Hugh O'Neill's followers, and all indulgences granted by previous Popes to Crusaders fighting against the Turks. A similar Indulgence was granted in 1580 by Pope Gregory XIII to the Earl of Desmond's followers, and these two documents give us a fair idea of the opinion which those Popes held of the English at those periods.

It is not surprising to find that at this time about a dozen of the McCarthys of Kilcoe and elsewhere, as many more of the O'Driscolls, as well as Connor O'Mahony of Leamcon, and many others, left Ireland permanently for Spain, and there started the first Irish Brigade. Amongst the O'Driscolls who so departed were Sir Fineen's two sons Conogher (the eldest) and Donnell, and his grandson Connor Oge aged 9 (son of Conogher), also Dermod O'Driscoll of

Castlehaven with his brother and sons, and a son of Gilliduff O'Driscoll of Cape Clear.

Carew tells us that, after the fighting ceased, he caused Beare, Bantry and Carbery to be left absolutely wasted, constraining all the inhabitants to withdraw their cattle into East and North Cork, to prevent supplies being available for a further rising. And then his work complete he left for England, in March 1603, where he was loaded with titles and honours which he did not live long to enjoy, and he was buried in Stratford-on-Avon.

Carew was succeeded as Lord President of Munster, in 1604, by Sir Henry Becher, son of Fane Becher, and it was either he or his son, another Henry, who moved from Bandon to West Carbery, and it appears that as early as 1618 Henry obtained a lease of some property in or around Baltimore, so he must have been in that district in or prior to that year, and a little later we find him the owner of lands in Sherkin and Ringarogy. The 2nd Henry Becher by Deed dated 2nd May 1619 conveyed the portion of Bandon Town which lies south of the river to the Earl of Cork.

CHAPTER VIII

AFTERMATH OF THE REBELLION

Following the rebellion there were the usual confiscations of property in West Carbery, but they seem to have been on a very light scale, and nothing like the sweeping ones which followed later risings. Castlehaven Castle, and the lands round it known as Glenbarrahane, were granted to George Touchet, Lord Audley, an Englishman, who later, in 1616, was created Earl of Castlehaven, but it will be remembered that the O'Driscoll owners of Castlehaven had gone to Spain, so these lands had no owner in occupation. Touchet's son, the 2nd Earl, came to a bad end, as in 1631 he was tried in England by his peers, and convicted of having committed some abominable crimes, and he was executed on Tower Hill. The title of Earl of Castlehaven became extinct in 1777 on the death of the 8th Earl without issue. But the Audley family continued as owners of this property up to 1852, when it was sold, in the Estate of George, Lord Baron Audley, by the Incumbered Estates Court, to Thomas Somerville, whose grandson, the late Colonel Somerville, sold it to the tenants under the Land Acts.

Sir Thomas Crooke, an Englishman, described as of "Donnesheade", also obtained a Crown Grant of Baltimore, with its castle and surrounding lands, and lands in the islands of Clear, Sherkin, Ringarogy and Innisbeg, formerly belonging to the O'Driscolls and the right to hold, in Baltimore, a market every Thursday and fairs on 9 days. It is well to add that a market had existed in Baltimore long before that time. An English settlement was established in the town, it is said round the Cove, but broadly speaking neither the O'Driscolls, the O'Mahonys, the O'Donovans nor the McCarthys were actually disturbed to any great extent. It seems that Sir Henry Becher gave a temporary letting to Sir Fineen as, at the Assizes of March 1604, "Fyrmyn O'Driscoll of Dunoshee, Knight" is entered for £500 bond on the following condition "Whereas the castles of Donoshee and Donolonge by special Warrant from the Lord President, by Order of the Privy Council of England, are to be delivered into the possession of the above Sir Fyrmyn O'Driscoll, to inhabit and possess as a good subject, and also in 21 days after warning to deliver them up in good condition without waste or ruin." This arrangement cannot have lasted very long having regard to the Grant to Crooke and the dealings mentioned later on.

From an Inquisition held at Rosscarbery on 8th April, in the 6th year of King James I, (which some quote as the year 1608 and others 1609), and presided over by William Lyon, the first Protestant Bishop of the United Diocese of Cork, Cloyne and Ross, which became united in 1583, we get information strongly suggesting that Crooke obtained a Conveyance of Collymore from Sir Fineen before he obtained his Crown Grant, and further that Sir Fineen was not as honest in his dealings with his relatives as he might have been.

The Record states that there were produced at the Inquisition a Deed from Sir Fineen, his wife Ellen, and Walter Goolde, merchant, of Cork, who was probably a mortgagee, conveying to Crooke all Collymore, and demesne lands of 35¼ ploughlands, together with a Power of Attorney, dated 1st August 1600, from the 3 grantors to Edmond Knapp, to give possession of the lands to Crooke, which was an essential item of conveyancing in those days. It was after this Deed that Crooke surrendered his estate to the Crown and obtained a new Grant in lieu thereof.

Another Deed was produced from Donald McCarthy Reagh to Sir James Lancaster, London, dated 19th February 1605, of all Collymore, and a Power to Attorney, dated 3rd May 1606, from Lancaster to Crooke, to dispose of the property as his will and pleasure. This Deed suggests a

Conveyance of McCarthy Reagh's rights as overlord.

We next learn from the Inquisition that Sir Fineen and his second cousin Conogher formerly held most of the O'Driscoll lands, rents, and port dues in equal shares, and that Sir Fineen occupied Dunasead and Conogher occupied Dunalong; but that, Conogher's death, Sir Fineen calmly seized the entire estate and ousted Conogher's son, Fineen Carragh (meaning spotted) O'Driscoll who sued Sir Fineen for his loss. The case was left to the arbitration of Sir Walter Coppinger of Clohane, and John Meade of Cork, who decided that Sir Fineen was to have the entire property for his life, save a living for Carragh, who was to have the entire property for his life after Sir Fineen's death, save a living for Sir Fineen's son, and after the death of both litigants their respective heirs were to take the property equally. Fineen Carragh died first, and his son and heir, Donogh Carragh, then sued Sir Fineen and again the case went to arbitration, the arbitrators this time being Coppinger and Donnell O'Donovan of Castle Donovan. Their decision was that Sir Fineen was to get, solely and absolutely, Baltimore town and Dunasead Castle, also Ballyhinchy, Rath, Lackaghane, Munnig, Ballyisland with the castle at Lough Hyne, and some other lands and also half the O'Driscoll chief rents. Donogh was to get, solely and absolutely, Dunalong Castle, Slievemore (Sherkin) and Innisbeg, also land in Cape Clear and Ringarogy, etc. Sir Fineen had mortgaged Innisbeg and he was directed to pay this off and free it for Donogh. We may mention that Sir Fineen's mother was Jane O'Mahony, and his wife was a daughter of Sir Owen McCarthy Reagh.

About this time there appear on the scene two remarkable men who, starting with nothing, within a few years acquired enormous estates. The first is Richard Boyle, a lawyer, who came from England to Cork about the same time as Fane Becher, 1586, with only a few pounds in his pocket and some jewellery and clothes, as he himself declared, yet within 40 years became an Earl, and is known to posterity as the Great Earl of Cork, and he succeeded in becoming the owner of half of Munster. One of his sons became the Earl of Orrery, and at the end of the 17th Century was the owner of the tithes of Skibbereen. The Great Earl seems to have always managed to be on the winning side (changing sides when necessary!) and he accumulated so much wealth that when he was fined £15,000. for some offence by the then Deputy, Lord Wentworth, (afterwards Earl of Stafford who was beheaded by Charles I), he paid this huge sum with ease. He was also able to give costly presents of gold and jewels, and we are told that his wife's petticoat cost £35! The Earl is of interest to our story only so far as to mention that, in 1615, he seized some lands of the O'Mahonys near Ballydehob, under an alleged title, but he failed to hold same, and it was he who, in 1613, procured Town Charters for Clonakilty and the newly established English settlement at Baltimore town. Under these Charters each town became self governing under a Sovereign, 12 burgesses and a commonalty, and each town was represented in Parliament by 2 members. These privileges lasted till 1800, when they were abolished by law, and the owners of the town were paid compensation for their loss of the Charters and consequent patronage. Sir John Evans Freke was the the owner of Baltimore, and he received £15,000. compensation from the Government. He later became Baron Carbery, a title which was first created in 1715 by King George I.

The first M.P. for Baltimore was Sir Thomas Crooke, already mentioned, who sat in 1613. Later, Colonel Richard Townsend of Castletownshend, and Colonel Thomas Becher of Sherkin, (both of whom will again appear in our story), sat in 1661 and 1692 respectively, and various members of the Freke and Becher families sat subsequently. Jeremy O'Donovan, chief of Clan Loughlin, sat in 1689, and George

Evans in 1797, was the last M.P., while Richard Tonson held the long distance record by representing Baltimore as M.P. for 46 years from 1727.

It will be observed that Skibbereen was not mentioned at all by Carew in *Pacata Hibernia*, even though his army must have passed through the site of the town on its way to attack Lettertinlish. Furthermore, Skibbereen never received a Town Charter. These facts corroborate the belief that Skibbereen, if it existed at all, was a mere hamlet until after the Algerine raid on Baltimore which we shall relate in the next chapter.

The second remarkable man, to whom we have already referred, is Sir Walter Coppinger, sprung from an old Danish family, whose early history we have not got, but it is alleged that in his younger days he was a valet, or page, to Sir Fineen O'Driscoll, but later a merchant in Cork. In a letter written by Carew in 1600 he refers to "one called Coppinger sometime a footman to Sir Walter Raleigh" but it is not certain that he was the same person as Sir Walter Coppinger. He first appears in our story in 1601, as previously related, as, presumably, it was he who guided the English raiding party to Kilcoe. But he had previously acquired lands at Clohane and Lissangle, with the castle thereon known as "Cloghan Castle", (the same name as that at Lough Hyne), of which only a fragment now remains. This castle and the lands belonged to the McCarthys but, owing to the attainder of Donald McCarthy in 1573, as already mentioned, they were confiscated. Four years later the Government granted them to Sir Cormac McTeighe McCarthy whose 2 sons, after his death, conveyed them to Sir Walter, by Deed dated 16th May, 1594, and, as he held them during the years 1600 to 1603, it seems unlikely that it was this Castle of Cloghan which was captured by Carew's men, seeing the help Sir Walter gave the English in 1601. After the rebellion Sir Walter proceeded to accumulate enormous landed estates in

West Carbery, and it is not clear whether he did so solely for himself, or to cover up some chiefs not in good repute with the Government, and , if the latter, whether he played the game with the chiefs, but he seems to have collected lands formerly belonging to the 4 great clans of West Carbery.

First, in 1608, we find him obtaining a Conveyance from Donogh O'Driscoll (Dunalong) for £300., of Baltimore Castle and 16½ ploughlands, including Rath, Lackaghane, Munnig, Tullagh and Highfield; and one wonders was Donogh trying by this Deed to double-cross Sir Fineen?

Next, in 1610, Sir Thomas Crooke was granted a licence to convey to Sir Fineen, Sir Walter, and Donogh O'Driscoll the whole of Collymore, otherwise O'Driscolls country, with the Port of Baltimore, Cape Clear, Donegal and Sherkin. It will be recollected that 10 years earlier Sir Fineen had conveyed Collymore and other lands to Crooke.

The same year (1610), a lease was made by Crooke, Sir Fineen and Sir Walter to Thomas Bennett (Bandon), whose father, another Thomas, was one of the original colonists of Bandon under Fane Becher, for 21 years, of Baltimore and some lands near it, and, subject thereto, Crooke, the same year, conveyed all his lands to Sir Walter, and it is stated in this Deed that the conveyance was made with Sir Fineen's consent. Subsequently, in the reign of Charles I, an Inquisition was held in Bandon, where it was found as a fact that in 1611 a Fine was levied by Sir Fineen, his wife and Crooke in favour of Sir Walter, a Fine being an ancient method of conveying lands. Next, in 1612, another Grant was made by Crooke to Sir Walter which apparently was a mere confirmation. Why there was the necessity of making so many conveyances is not clear but at that time forgeries were common and presumably Sir Walter was taking no risks.

In 1612 Murtagh O'Driscoll mortgaged his castle and lands of Oldcourt and Derrygereen to Sir Walter for £60., and in 1630 Dermott O'Driscoll of Oldcourt created a further mortgage to him for £40.

In 1614 Sir Walter surrendered his estates to the King, and the following day received from the King a fresh Grant of the Manor of Cloghanemore, which included Cloghane, Cullinagh, Adrigole, Shreelane, and, in fact, most of the townlands round Skibbereen (though not Abbeystrowery etc. forming Skibbereen, no doubt because same belonged to McCarthy Reagh). Sir Walter was also granted the Manor of Kilfinnan, which included Kilfinnan, Drombeg etc. and he also got half of the Castle and lands of Rincolisky, half of the islands of Innishodriscoll or Hare Island, and East "Inishcame" (now Skeam), as well as many other lands in the Aughadown district. Finally this Grant also gave him Chief Rents out of many lands including Lettertinlish and Smorane.

In 1615 Sir Walter received another Crown Grant of Leamcon, Dromig, Dunmanus, Skeagh, and immense other tracts of land in West Carbery, and some more chief rents.

In 1618 William Barrett mortgaged Ballincolla (Union Hall) to Edmond Coppinger, who transferred same to Sir Walter in 1630, and the same year Barrett released to Sir Walter his equity of redemption, so Sir Walter became absolute owner of Ballincolla.

Before Crooke conveyed to Sir Walter, English settlers had come to Baltimore and, in 1618, James Spencer and others petitioned the Privy Council for relief against Sir Walter's Grant. The Petition claimed that Sir John Skinner, Thomas Crooke, and others had acquired lands in Carbery in order to "plant several colonies of English people and settle God's true religion and own subjection to His Majesty in those parts", but that Coppinger desired to supplant the Petitioners in their possessions, and that he had unlawfully acquired the lands by forgeries and other corrupt courses. The complaint was referred to 3 Commissioners, Sir William Hull, an Elizabethan settler, who was then Vice-Admiral of Munster, Henry Becher, already mentioned, who was the

father of Colonel Becher, and Mr. Barham. Sir Walter seems
to have made an arrangement with Becher, and gave him a
Lease, for which Sir Walter was confined to Dublin for con-
tempt of Court, and Becher was reprimanded, but his friend,
the Great Earl of Cork, got his lease confirmed. In the result,
the Petitioners do not seem to have received much help or
satisfaction.

In 1628 there was a dispute between Sir Walter and Sir
Fineen as to whether a certain Conveyance (presumably the
Fine of 1611) was an absolute conveyance, as alleged by Sir
Walter, or a mortgage, as alleged by Sir Fineen. Chancery
proceedings followed and the suit was referred to 4 arbitra-
tors, Donnell O'Donovan of Raheen being one. During the Suit
Donogh, son and agent of Sir Fineen, slandered Sir Walter.
The Arbitrators, in their Award dated 13th April, 1629,
found that Sir Walter had given Sir Fineen £1693.0.1. which
they directed should be redeemed for £1300., owing to Sir
Fineen's "decrepide" age and want of means, and that Sir
Walter should have the property, and on payment to him
of £1300. should give a Deed of Defeasance (i.e. Release) to
Sir Fineen, who was directed to apologise to Sir Walter for
Donogh's slander. The Defeasance Deed is dated 14th April,
1629 and was made between Sir Walter Coppinger of
Cloghane Knt. and Sir Fynin O'Driscoll of Bally Island, Knt.

It is unknown when or where Sir Fineen died, but
probably it was soon after this and at Cloghan Castle in
Lough Hyne. He must have been a very old man as he
became chieftain in 1573.

Next we find Sir Walter, in 1636, making what appears
to be a renewal lease to Thomas Bennett of Bandon of the
Castle and Village of Baltimore with some land adjoining
same.

These various transactions are not easy to understand or
reconcile, but they do suggest that Sir Walter acquired Sir
Fineen's estate legally and for value, and no proceedings were

afterwards brought against the Coppingers by the O'Driscolls, similar to those brought against Colonel Becher which we shall describe later. They also suggest that, even if the confiscations after 1603 were nominally extensive, Sir Walter saved actual disturbance of the owners, and he must have restored much of the property he acquired to the original owners as we find Donogh O'Driscoll (Carragh) in possession of a considerable part of O' Driscoll territory until after the rebellion of 1641, while Denis O'Driscoll occupied Oldcourt as late as 1700. Also we find the O'Mahonys still in possession of Leamcon and Dunmanus, and making leases of some of their land in 1622 to Sir William Hull.

In Smith's History of Cork an interesting story is told of how Sir Fineen, after the rebellion, tried to get back to favour with the English. It appears an English fleet came into Baltimore Harbour, and Sir Fineen lavishly entertained the officers, and to amuse them, and enrich the sailors, he flooded the town well (over which there is now a pump) with wine, and threw handfuls of money in it, so that the well is still known as Tober-an-arigid (the well of money). On hearing this, Queen Elizabeth pardoned Sir Fineen for having joined the Spaniards, and she sent for him to attend at her Court, but she died before his arrival. Perhaps it was this entertainment which caused the financial difficulties in which we find Sir Fineen in his old age?

But Sir Walter, whatever property he gave away, kept much of it for himself and he seems to have become a very wealthy man, and early in the 17th century he built Coppinger's Court, which stands between Glandore and Rosscarbery. Anyone viewing the ruins today will realise that the building was intended to accommodate a large number of people and cost a considerable sum to erect. This building is of interest to show the change in architecture which took place in Queen Elizabeth's reign when the fortified house succeeded the Norman Castle. The latter must have been

Coppinger's Court

expensive to build, and uncomfortable to live in, and the coming of firearms into Ireland, about 1500 AD, showed that the Castles were not even places of safety, so the building of them fell into disuse early in the 17th Century.

Coppinger's Court had the reputation, at that time, of being the largest house in Carbery, and had, it is said, a door for every week, a chimney for every month and a window for every day of the year.

Tradition says that Sir Walter was a tyrant, and that he had a permanent gallows attached to his house for hanging those who offended him. It is also said that on the day of his death he had arranged to hang someone, but it being Sunday he went to his devotions first, and on leaving the Church he dropped dead in a fit, which the local people considered a visitation of Providence.

During the rebellion of 1641 Coppinger's Court was attacked and partially burnt down by the rebels.

In a later part of our story we shall meet with two sons of Sir Walter, Domenick and Thomas, and a brother Richard, as well as some others of his descendants.

We may add that the Coppinger burying place was in Christ Church, Cork.

CHAPTER IX

THE SACK OF BALTIMORE AND
THE REBELLION OF 1641

The next event of importance in West Carbery is the Algerine raid on Baltimore, on the night of 20th June, 1631, but Thomas Davis seems to have relied on his imagination rather than on facts when composing his famous poem "The Sack of Baltimore", as Joseph Carter, Sovereign of Baltimore, 7 days after the event, wrote to Sir William Hull reporting the attack, and he said that only 2 people had been killed, and 111 taken away, whose names are given and suggest that they were the English folk who had settled round the Cove. The poet's romantic story of the capture of O'Driscoll's daughter in Dunasead also seems to have had no foundation in fact, because, as we have seen, Thomas Bennett was at that time the lessee of the Castle, and he remained in occupation for many years later.

The raiders came in 2 Turkish ships, one of 300 tons and the other of 150. Hackett of Dungarvan, a fisherman, whom they took off a boat, piloted them. He was later executed in Cork for doing so, though he seems to have had no option in the matter of the piloting.

It seems curious that these ships should come such a long distance to such a small place without having had first hand information about Baltimore, so perhaps we are justified in assuming that this information came from the O'Driscoll emigrés in Spain who, in this way, sought for revenge on the English who had driven them out. Probably the raiders were told glowing tales of the wealth of the place, and this not materializing, they took persons instead of gold, in the hope of obtaining fat ransoms for them, which they do not seem to have got.

But it is claimed that the raid produced two important results, namely, the founding of the town of Skibbereen by refugees from the Baltimore district, who were determined not to be attacked again from the sea and, secondly, the English King, Charles I, fearing such raids might be repeated in other parts of the British Isles, proceeded to levy Ship Money to equip his Navy, which produced such opposition that it eventually led to the Civil War in England, the beheading of Charles himself and the raising of Cromwell to power as Protector of the English Commonwealth.

The Algerines were not the only pirates which then haunted our coasts, for we are told that in May 1631 another buccaneer called Nut, with his fleet of 3 ships, anchored in Crookhaven for provisions and, though offered a free pardon by the Government, he was quite reluctant to accept it. It is said that Nut used to bury his plunder on various headlands, sacrificing a black slave at each place whose spirit was to watch over the treasure. It is also said that Sir William Hull, though Vice-Admiral of the district, was not above trading with Nut, and with a Dutch pirate named Campane who anchored in Leamcon Harbour in 1624.

King Charles was chronically hard up and would do, or promise to do, anything to get money. Knowing this, the English and Irish in Ireland offered him a large sum of money in return for certain concessions, or "graces" as they were called. The King accepted the bargain, took the money, but failed to give the "graces", one of the principal of which was that 60 years title without flaw gave the holder an absolute title to his lands. The withholding of the "graces" was one of the causes which brought about the rising of 1641, called in some legal documents, made after the restoration of Charles II as King, the "horrid rebellion".

The rising was fixed for 23rd October, 1641, and again an Irish traitor, Colonel Owen O'Connolly, in a half drunken condition, gave warning to the English and enabled them to avoid a surprise attack. For this service, the Act of Settlement of 1662 provided that lands in Co. Dublin to the value of £200. per year were to be given to his two orphan children Arthur and Martha. The insurrection did not spread to Munster until a month later, and Cork was the very last County in Ireland to rise, Glandore being the place where it began. The first Irishman was killed by Arthur Freke's men near Rathbarry Castle (Castlefreke) in January 1642, and the first Englishman was killed, early the next month, when 3 men, returning from Rathbarry to Glandore,Castle, then held by Colonel Samuel Salmon, were ambushed, and one was killed and the other 2 wounded.

We get some interesting information from a fragment of a report written by an unknown local person. He says:—"On May Eve (1641) I came from Cork to my own house at Rosscarbery where I met with Domenick Coppinger Esq. (son of Sir Walter) who came to entreat me to dine with him the morrow after at his house in Ballinvreine (Coppinger's Court), and desired that my man might bring a musket to help to bring home the May, and set up a May Pole at his new intended plantation by the Roury Bridge, where he had begun the foundation of a market house, a mile from Ross. The former I refused, the latter I sent him". The same writer tells us that about 20th November, 1641 McCarthy Reagh O'Donovan, Domenick Coppinger J.P., his brother Thomas (another J.P.), Teighe O'Driscoll who married their sister, Donogh Carragh O'Driscoll, Florence McCarthy of Benduff, Rickard O'Donovan of Kilfinnan, and other McCarthys and O'Donovans were summoned by McCarthy, Lord of the country, to appear to raise a force to defend the western parts, hearing there was a rebellion in East Munster. Finally, we learn that the writer, on 2nd January, 1642, fled to Rathbarry Castle for safety, having been warned of his danger

by Teighe O'Downy. As we shall see later, several of the
chiefs named above afterwards took an active part in the
rising, including McCarthy Reagh, Tom Coppinger, Teighe
O'Driscoll, O'Donovan and Florence McCarthy of Benduff,
but Domenick Coppinger did not.

In September 1642 a temporary truce was arranged
under which the English were to retain part of County Cork,
including the portion between Youghal and Fermoy to
Bandon and Timoleague, but the rest, including all of West
Carbery, was to be held by the Irish.

During the rising frightful atrocities and destruction
were committed on both sides, and even the rack as a form of
torture was used by the English on the Irish captives in
Dublin Castle. The fighting did not finally cease until 1652
under the iron rule of Cromwell. The rebellion at one time
developed many sides and parties, which gradually merged
into Cromwell and his Parliamentarians against the rest, but
this belongs to general history and does not materially affect
our story.

In this rebellion, unfortunately, we have no historian
like Carew to give us in detail what happened in West Carbery,
but it seems fairly certain that all the 4 great clans joined
some party in the rising and all suffered in the result.

About the O'Mahonys (then under the leadership of
Conner O'Mahony who lived in Ballydevlin Castle, Goleen),
we have the information that they beseiged Sir William Hull
in Crookhaven, and his son in Leamcon, so the settlers left
on an English ship, as did also the occupant of Rossbrin
Castle (forfeited after the Desmond rebellion) and other
planters. After the rebellion most of the O'Mahonys were
outlawed, and lost their lands, and probably went to Spain,
but the Hulls returned and they continued to occupy land in
the Schull district up to our own time. After the O'Mahony
confiscations the English for a time used Crookhaven as a
prison, and we may add that, after the execution of Charles I,

his nephew Prince Rupert, on his way to Kinsale with the royal fleet, put into Crookhaven Harbour, owing to the mistake of his pilot.

Sir William Hull appears to have fled to Bandon, for in 1642 numerous depositions were taken at Bandon of losses sustained by loyalists, and he made one himself, and claimed a total loss of £7679. (a very large sum in those days), besides the value of his fee simple lands which produced £183. per year, and his leasehold lands and mortgages estimated at £1065. per year. He also stated that Captain Cole, who commanded the ship which rescued himself and his son before leaving the district, burned the towns of Crookhaven and Schull, which then belonged to Hull.

Another deposition, made by George Fenton, Merchant, of Bandon, claimed the loss of debts amounting to £1505., and, amongst a long list of debtors, we find the following names which are of interest to us:- Rickard O'Donovan of Castle Donovan, Florence McCarthy of Benduff, Thomas Coppinger of Rincolisky, Daniel O'Sullivan Bere and his brother, and a number of other McCarthys. The claimant must have been doing a big business to have debtors from such varied and distant places with such poor transport and roads as then existed. Anne Taylor of Bandon also claimed the loss of £47. due to her by Daniel O'Donovan of Castle Donovan.

As regards the O'Driscolls, we find that, on 15th August 1642, Teighe O'Driscoll of Collymore and Dermod O'Driscoll of Innisherkin, with 200 men, joined Tom Coppinger of Collybeg, with 100 men, and attacked Baltimore Castle. Bennett was governor of the Castle and he gave shelter to 215 of the townsfolk. The O'Driscolls had 40 muskets and 4 rounds of ammunition for each, and Coppinger had 30 muskets. They attacked 3 times before daybreak but were beaten off, and we are told that no-one was hurt. Bennett continued to hold the Castle until 1645 when he yielded it to

Cromwell's men. After the rebellion Donogh and Cornelius
O'Driscoll both of Dunalong, Teighe and Florence (alias
Fineen) O'Driscoll of Ballymacrown, Dermot O'Driscoll of
Oldcourt, and others of the same clan were outlawed and
their estates were confiscated.

About the O'Donovans, Rev. Urbanus Vigors, whose
father, Rev. Louis Vigors, lived in Rosscarbery, writing in
1642 says the "Great O'Donovan" (presumably Donnell, the
then chief of Clan Cahill, who about 2 years earlier had
adopted the title of O'Donovan of Castledonovan and
Bawnlahan) "did much spoil about the Leape, Castlehaven,
Bantry, Rosscarbery, and divers other places". He also says
that "Great O'Donovan's" father was a most notorious rebel
who had burnt the town of Ross during the last war, and he
or his men had killed a deaf and dumb daughter of Bishop
Lyon, but by coming in on protection he saved his land. The
writer further tells us that the rebels used the Cathedral of
Ross as a slaughter house, and, finally, that "O'Sullivan
Beare, Teighe O'Donnce, Florence McCarthy of the Castle
of Benduff, Black O'Cullane, and other freeholders near Ross
joined forces and took a great store of pillage and robbed the
English about Bantry, Kilcoe, Affadowne, Balledehab,
Landore, Cloghnakilty, Inniskeame, Castletowne, the town of
Ross and all those parts".

From another source we learn that Donnell O'Donovan
was a man distinguished both in war and peace, admired by
his friends, and respected by his enemies, and that he died in
1660. He was a strict royalist, and joined the 3rd Earl of
Castlehaven, who was one of the chief leaders of the royalists
in Ireland, in the struggle against Cromwell, and both lost
their estates when Cromwell triumphed. During the fighting
about 1649/1650 Donnell's two castles at Castledonovan
(Drimoleague) and Raheen (Union Hall) were attacked and
captured by Cromwell's men and then blown up. In Raheen
Castle are still to be seen the marks of cannon balls, fired

it is thought from ships in Castlehaven Harbour.

It is not certain that Cromwell himself ever entered West Carbery, though there is a tradition that he did, and that he spent one night in Abbeystrowery, and that he was present when O'Donovan's castles were blown up.

The McCarthys also joined in the rebellion, headed by Daniel McCormac McCarthy Reagh, who was High Sheriff of County Cork in 1635. He applied to Lord Kinalmeaky (son of the Great Earl of Cork) for arms to fight for the English, and, having obtained them, he marched to attack the pro-English town of Bandon, but he was defeated, and soon after his castle at Kilbrittain was taken from him and he became a fugitive.

To the credit of the McCarthys, it is admitted that they did their best to prevent atrocities by their followers, but they suffered the fate of the other rebels and all their great estates were confiscated.

It is recorded that on 11th July, 1650 Daniel O'Donovan, Donnogh McDaniel McCarthy and F. O'Driscoll signed a pact for mutual protection against oppression to defend their property, the vote of the majority to rule, but it came too late to save them.

Arthur Freke has written a detailed account of the happenings in Rathbarry Castle during the year 1642, and of the siege and attacks on the Castle, until, in October, he and the other inmates were relieved and carried off by the English Army. In July 1642, during the siege, a boat was built in Rathbarry Castle of barrel boards, and 4 men rowed in it to Castlehaven hoping to find an English ship to bring help to the garrison, but failing to find one they went into Glandore Harbour where they found Captain Brown of the "Elizabeth" of Plymouth who, in his long boats, came to Castlefreke and evacuated the women and children, and some of the men, to Kinsale.

We also learn from this Freke report that during the

siege Rev. Taverner, the Protestant clergyman, was removed from Rathbarry to Baltimore, where the previous incumbent had died, so evidently the Protestant clergy were not interfered with during the rising.

The report suggests that the fighting in that district was on a small scale, but with frequent skirmishes and ambushes. Before the garrison left, the Castle and houses and contents were set on fire by the relieving army, and the ruins of the castle can still be seen in Castlefreke demesne.

CHAPTER X

AFTERMATH OF THE REBELLION

Certainly Cromwell can never be accused of doing things by halves. His confiscations were so thorough that they ran from the 3 acres of Catherine Quirke in Galway to the 100,000. acres of the Lord of Muskerry. Though, after the Restoration of the Monarchy, in 1660, some of the land owners recovered some or all of their estates the small proprietors disappeared completely. For the purpose of these confiscations Cromwell directed a Survey to be made of all Ireland, which was done in 1653 by Sir William Petty, and is known as the *Down Survey*. For this work he was only paid one penny per acre. It is a national loss that this valuable Record was destroyed in the Four Courts fire in 1922.

Grants of forfeited lands were then handed out broadcast to Cromwell's officers and men. Many of the grantees did not take up their allotments but sold them, or gave or gambled them away, and left the country. On the other hand, a few men of long vision and considerable courage collected these lots and so acquired large estates.

In 1662 the "Act of Settlement" was passed, confirming the new settlers in their lands, but it set up a Court of Claims, which sat in 1663 in the King's Inns, Dublin, to which Catholics who had no connection with the rising of 1641 could apply for a Decree that they were "Innocent Papists" and, if they succeeded, they were to get back their lands, and the new settlers were to get land elsewhere. All dispossessed Protestants were also to be restored. Later, in 1665, the "Act of Explanation" was passed under which the new settlers need only give up one third of their possessions to restored owners, and a new Court of Claims under this Act sat in 1666 to issue Patents and Certificates to those entitled.

Some of these grants are of special interest to our story, as follows:—

1.   Sir Algernon May and Dame Dorothy his wife received 2 ploughlands of Donegall and one other ploughland, all in Ringarogy Island, 3 ploughlands of Dunalong (Sherkin), Munig, Croha (Cape Clear), and "Glantagh" wherever that may be. All of these were formerly O'Driscoll territory. These lands were afterwards sold in 1675 for £1400. by the grantees to Colonel Thomas Becher, grandson of Sir Henry.

2.   Colonel Richard Townsend received, either by grant or purchase, other O'Driscoll lands, consisting of one ploughland and 8 greeves of Slievemore (Sherkin), another 1½ ploughlands of Ringarogy and ½ a ploughland of "Gortaculkah" wherever that may be, and these lands he sold to Colonel Becher for £250.

3.   In addition to the above, Colonel Townsend collected by direct grant, or otherwise, a very large estate, comprising 41 townlands, as widely scattered as Dunbeacon (Durrus), Coronea (including the part of Skibbereen known as Bridgetown to the west of the Keal) and Gortbrack (Castletownshend), which included parts of the old territory of all four of the chief tribes of West Carbery. He received Patents for these lands as we shall see later.

4.   The Becher family still have in their possession the original Patent made by Charles II on 17th July, 1668 to Henry Becher (father of the Colonel), Thomas Becher, and John Brayly, of Dromore, and of other lands outside West Carbery, unless "Curran" mentioned therein is the modern Garrane (Caheragh). This document is in English, and in excellent condition, and contains at the top a painting of the "Merry Monarch" himself. It is of interest to mention that one of the Commissioners who gave the Certificate for this Patent was Sir Winston Churchill, Knight, father of the famous Duke of Marlborough.

5.   William Prigg and Samuel Hall about 1670 were granted the lands of Gortnaclohy (including the portion of Skibbereen to the east of the Keal) which was then proposed

to be called New Stapleton. They sold part of their grant to Colonel Becher, and the rest passed into the ownership of the Estate of "Townsend and Wright" under a Deed dated 22nd June, 1761 made by Dublin bankers.

And now let us see how the 4 great tribes fared under the Acts of Settlement and Explanation. It seems that the O'Mahonys disappeared and failed to get back any of their lands.

Colonel Charles McCarthy Reagh was to be restored to his chief house, and 2,000. acres adjoining, but Cromwellian grantees had got too firm a hold, and in 1666 not an acre in Carbery remained to the family.

After the death of Donnell O'Donovan, his son, Daniel of Clan Cahill, succeeded in getting back part of his manor of Raheen (which did not include Castle Ire as Colonel Townsend got this). O'Donovan, however, lost his manor of Castledonovan which was granted to Lieutenant Nathaniel Evanson.

Jeremy O'Donovan of Clan Loughlin (who as previously mentioned was M.P. for Baltimore in 1689) also got a Patent for Keamore (Leap) after he had bought it back from Colonel Townsend.

The O'Donovans also, between 1629 and 1670, obtained Conveyances from the O'Driscolls of Ardagh and Ballinard (Baltimore), and also acquired from the O'Driscolls Lick, Bunlick and Gortshanecrone (Skibbereen).

As regards the O'Driscolls, we get some very interesting information from 2 ancient documents still extant. First there is the Administration with the Will annexed of "Donogh O'Driscoll alias Carragh", who died in 1647, and whom we have already referred to. The parchment copy of the Will is damaged in places and therefore difficult to read. It is in English, and dated 5th March, 1644, with a Postscript, or as we would say a Codicil, dated 10th March, 1644. Both documents are witnessed by Cahir O'Thohig, Parish Priest,

Daniel Callanane and Teige O'Riogayne. The attached
Administration, also on parchment, is in Latin, and was
issued on 6th July 1670 to Tadeain (Latin for Teighe)
O'Driscoll, son of the testator, by Edward Synge, Protestant
Bishop of Cork, Cloyne and Ross, as in those days all
Probates and Administrations were issued by the Church.
The testator commenced by directing his body to be buried
in the Abbey of "Inishurkane" where his daughters were
buried. It seems curious that now there is no trace in the
Abbey of the O'Driscoll tomb or graves, nor even any
tradition of the locality. The Testator then devised his
freehold lands which descended to him from his ancestors to
his son Conogher (who predeceased him). However, he
excepted one ploughland and 8 greeves of Slievemore
(presumably those already mentioned which were given to
Colonel Townsend), the Castle and lands of Dunanore and
other lands, in Cape Clear, all of which he gave to his said son
Teighe in tail male, subject to his paying the old O'Driscoll
chief rents to the testator's chief heir. His son, Dermod, got
2 small mortgages of £12. and £10. on local lands, and his
son, Daniel, a mortgage of £10. Teighe was directed to pay
his sister, "Eillyne", £20. and to his sister, Hanora, £10. but
the former was also to get three score pounds from her
brother, Conogher, as well as 6 young cows out of testator's
moveables, the rest of which he gave to his wife and children
for maintenance. The testator seems to have had a very
dubious opinion of the honesty of his father-in-law, Richard
Coppinger, (brother of Sir Walter), for he gave him 1½
ploughlands in Ringarogy for life "for mere love and
affection and for no other consideration" and he added the
following tag "moreover he enjoys another half ploughland in
Reenaroga aforesaid without any color or consideration, all
which I protest is true, so that he cannot challenge no other
title that may disinherit my heir of the same". On reflection
he seems to have thought this a bit too hard on his father-in-

law, for 5 days later he added a "Postscript" in which he speaks of "the good service that the said Richard hath done unto me in my lifetime in many places within this Kingdom of Ireland", and in consideration thereof he gave him £100. charged on the said lands in Ringarogy, and also gave him absolutely a parcel of land called "Mealebracke" at Gortnalicky, also in Ringarogy.

Richard Coppinger was outlawed after the rebellion. He made his Will on 16th April, 1651, and he devised Dunanore (Cape Clear) to his grandchild, Teighe O'Driscoll, and directed that he should be buried in Sherkin Abbey, but we do not know whether this direction was carried out. It is also recorded that in 1634 a suit brought by James FitzEdmond FitzGerald against Richard Coppinger of Donegal was dismissed, and the latter was declared entitled to 3 gueeves called Liskanmaine (part of Creagh).

From the second document already mentioned, dated 1700, and to which we shall again refer later, we find that both Donogh and Conogher were dead when the Court of Claims sat in 1663, but Donogh Junior (son of Conogher) came before the Court and succeeded in proving that the 3 of them were "innocent papists". Instead of ordering possession of the lands to be given to Donogh Junior he was left to bring an action of ejectment against the Patentees of the lands, viz. Sir Algernon May and his wife and others. In the original claim Donogh Junior claimed that his grandfather, when the rebellion broke out, held in fee tail and that on his death Donogh Junior, as heir of Conogher, became entitled, but curiously enough the grandfather's Will is not referred to at all.

From a source other than the Becher document we learn that the O'Driscoll claim was made in a Petition presented by both Donogh Junior and his mother Catherine (born Carthy), and that the deceased Conogher resided in Donegal (Ringarogy) which was part of his wife's fortune. The

Petition stated that Catherine and her said son (then a minor) were "expulsed by the late usurped powers in or about the year 1654", and claimed that Donogh Senior, late of Dunalong, and the Petitioners behaved "civilly, innocently and inoffensively during the rebellion". The lands claimed were Sherkin and Donegal, then in the possession of Henry Becher, save part of Slievemore which was mortgaged to "Captain Jarvoys". At some later stage Colonel Cornelius O'Driscoll seems to have filed a Petition, the record of which is unperfect, in which he claimed Baltimore, Rath, Ballyisland, Creagh, Gorteenalomane, Lick, and other lands, about 2,400 acres in all, but we have not been able to trace the result of it.

To return to the Becher document, it is said that it is foolish to change horses when crossing a stream, but this we find Donogh Junior did, for in his ejectment action, brought in 1671, instead of the title already claimed, he pleaded a Deed of Settlement, made in 1633, in the 9th year of the reign of King Charles I, under which his grand-parents and parents became entitled for life only, with remainder to himself as his parents' eldest son. Colonel Becher was then a lessee from the Mays and defended the action, which was tried at Cork Assizes, and the Court found that the said Settlement was clearly a forgery, mainly it seems because the expression "King Charles I" was used therein, which expression could not have been used before the 2nd Charles came to the throne, which did not occur till many years after 1633. Donogh Junior was therefore non-suited which, under the Act of Explanation, was a perpetual bar to his claim.

But while West Cork brains over-reached themselves in the matter of the forged Deed they were not dead yet, because the O'Driscolls succeeded in stealing the Court records of the case, and then, in the year 1687, Cornelius O'Driscoll (son and heir of Donogh Junior who was then dead) brought another ejectment action against Colonel Becher for the lands he had bought from the Mays and Colonel Townsend. This action came for trial at the Cork Assizes in April, 1688. The country was again in a very disturbed state, and the religious question had become very acute during the reign of James II. Under threats of violence Becher settled the action by a written Agreement, dated 13th April, 1688, under which O'Driscoll was to get back all his lands, save a moiety of 4 ploughlands and 2 gueeves of Ringarogy, Slievemore, and "Glanmanash" (wherever that may be), until the title to same had been examined by Counsel. On the other hand, Becher was to get a Lease of a moiety of all the lands for 99 years, at the yearly rent of 6/8d. per ploughland. Becher had to pay £150. to O'Driscoll, and each side was to pay its own costs. O'Driscoll entered up Judgement, and under it evicted Becher, and then refused to make the agreed Lease.

Conditions in the country became more unsettled still and Becher and his wife and 7 children fled to England for safety at the end of 1688, and it is recorded that, at that time, his income was £898. per year.

Many other landowners left about the same time, including Percy Freke, to whom we shall refer, whose annual income was then £520.

And now we must leave O'Driscoll and Becher for a while to give a short account of Colonel Townsend.

He was a Colonel in Cromwell's army in England and he landed in Cork in 1647, and went through a good deal of the fighting in Munster. One modern writer suggests that he was a spy sent to Ireland by Cromwell to corrupt the Munster army, while professing hatred for the republicans. At any rate, it was he who informed Cromwell that Munster had submitted, and Cromwell then reported "I hear by Colonel Townsend that Baltimore, Castlehaven, and other places of hard names are come in".

About 1654 Townsend left the army and settled in
Castlehaven, and his family claim that he became so friendly
with his neighbours that the dispossessed McCarthy Reagh
made a Will in his favour, and that one of Townsend's sons
was named Cornelius, after one of the O'Driscolls who, on
one occasion, gave the Colonel's wife shelter and protection
when Castletownshend was attacked by an armed band and
she had to fly. In addition, Townsend married one of his
daughters, Dorothea, to Domenick Coppinger Junior to
whom we shall refer again. His eldest daughter, Hildigard, is
buried on Horse Island, off Castlehaven, and a standing stone
near the landing place on the north shore is said to be her
head stone.

About 1666 we find Townsend a Captain in a militia
raised for defence by the local gentry of Carbery, consisting
of 300 horse and 400 foot, and in the same force we meet
other well known local names such as Captain Richard Hull,
Captain John Freake, Ensign Francis Beamish, Lieutenant T.
Becher and Quarter-Master W. Baldwin. In 1666 also
Townsend obtained a Patent for 32 townlands (including
Bridgetown, Skibbereen), most of them in West Carbery, and
in 1688 he obtained another Patent for 17 townlands, 8 of
which were already in the earlier one so why they should be
repeated is unknown. Finally, in 1675, he obtained a 3rd
Patent for all his lands in Carbery (60 townlands then),
containing 8,000. acres, which were consolidated into one
manor under the name of Bridgetown *alias* Coronea. Many
of these lands, and others subsequently obtained, remained in
possession of the Townsend family until the year 1897, when
the entire estate, then containing over 10,000. acres, was sold
by the Land Judges Court in the Estate of Mrs. Geraldine
Henrietta Townsend Mundy.

There were numbers of other Patents granted by the
Court of Claims to ancestors of families well known to us,
such as Beamish, Becher, Cox, Fleming, Galwey, Hull,

Aftermath of the Rebellion

Hungerford, French and Morris.

The Coppinger Estates were also forfeited, owing to the rebellion, in the hands of Domenick Coppinger already mentioned, who died in 1642, and was a son of Sir Walter. His other son Tom was outlawed in addition. Domenick's widow, Mary, and son, James, claimed a return of Domenick's estates and the Court of Claims on 6th November, 1663 decreed that they, and also Domenick, were "Innocent Papists", and ordered that two thirds of the estates should be returned to James forthwith and the remaining one third after his mother's death. The restored estates contained in all 27,338. acres and included Rincolisky and Oldcourt. James died soon after, having by his Will, made on 27th November, 1665, devised all his property to his brother Walter. The Will mentions the Manor of Cloghanemore, also Rincolisky, Inane, Oldcourt, Inishodriscoll, "Inishcame", Cullinagh etc. The Coppingers must have had great influence at the time as the following letter from Cromwell to his son Henry shows:-

For the Lord Henry Cromwell.
Upon the addresses of James Coppinger Esq., finding that his case, if truly stated by the enclosed, to be different from many others, and in respect his father was faithful to the Parliament in assisting against the rebellion, and lending at the first £500. towards the maintenance of the army, and supplying it with victuals and other necessities, upon which account the rebels burned his house and his castles, and that he himself never acted against the Parliament, and hath lately married a gentlewoman who is a Protestant and of good repute, we desire that all favour may be shown him, both as to his estate and also in exempting him from transplantation and rest
Whitehall,   *Your loving father,*
14th August, 1655   *Oliver, P.*

73

But, like the Great Earl of Cork, James Coppinger managed to keep in with both sides, and Charles II in his Declaration, made on 30th November, 1660, (subsequently incorporated in the Act of Settlement of 1662) named him (amongst a number of other gentlemen) as having "for reasons known to us in an especial manner merited our grace and favour" and the Act directed them to be restored to their estates.

The same Declaration names "Colonel Charles MacCarty Rieagh of Kilbretan" and "Colonel Cornelius O'Driscol of Donesaide", and some other MacCarthys, O'Donovans and O'Driscolls of lesser military rank, as having served with the King beyond the seas, and therefore entitled to get back their lands, but some at least, and possibly all of them, were afterwards overlooked.

Under the Act James, Lord Audley, Earl of Castlehaven was also to get back his lands, and he got them, and his descendant remained the owner up to 1852 when, as previously mentioned, his estates were sold by the Court.

Doubtless Colonel O'Driscoll mentioned above is the same man who, as already stated, filed a Petition claiming Baltimore etc. and, judging by the lands claimed, he must have been a descendant of Sir Fineen.

CHAPTER XI

THE WAR OF 1689/1691

We now come to the war between King James II and King William III. King James landed at Kinsale on 12th March, 1689, and proceeded to Dublin via Cork. The peasants greeted him enthusiastically, with garlands of cabbage stalks, as laurels were not available. How different was his return journey to Kinsale, after the Battle of the Boyne, when he was given an unsavoury Irish nickname which has stuck to him for nearly 300 years.

But the Battle of the Boyne, the capture of Cork by John Churchill, afterwards Duke of Marlborough, and the sieges of Derry and Limerick belong to general history, and we are only concerned with such few items as are available about the happings in West Carbery.

First then, we find that Cornelius O'Driscoll of Dunalong became a Lieutenant Colonel in King James' Army, while his old enemy, Colonel Becher, who had come back from England, served in William's Army, and for his services at the Boyne the King presented him with a large silver watch which his family still have. A number of the O'Driscoll family seem to have served with King James as we are told that a Captain O'Driscoll served at the Boyne; but perhaps it was he who afterwards was promoted to the rank of Lieutenant Colonel?

Next, we are told that, on 2nd October 1689, the English stormed James' Fort, Kinsale, and, after the Governor, Colonel O'Driscoll, was killed, with several others, the fort surrendered.

Our next information comes from Story who tells us that, on 23rd November, 1689, "500 Irish, under young Colonel O'Driscoll, attempted to burn Castletown, the mansion house of Colonel Townsend in West Carbery, but they missed their aim and were so well received by him and his garrison, consisting of about 35 men, that 12 of them dropt at the first volley, and upon a 2nd attack, Driscoll, Captain Tieg Donovan, Captain Croneen, and about 30 others were slain, and so many others wounded that they were forced to retire with loss and shame. One, Captain Mac Ronaine, with his drawn sword, endeavoured to hinder his men's retreat, but he being killed they got away; several of them had bundles of straw on their breasts to resist the shot, but, notwithstanding, 30 were slain on the spot". As the Becher document of 1700 does not state Cornelius O'Driscoll of Dunalong was then dead it seems that the two Colonels O'Driscoll killed as above were other members of the clan.

Castletownsend was again attacked, in December 1690, by 400 men under MacFineen O'Driscoll who escaped from Cork jail. After 5 of the garrison of 39 dragoons had been killed the rest were forced to surrender. Later Colonel Culliford retook the Castle, after killing 10, and capturing 10, of the Jacobite garrison. These sieges so damaged his mansion that the Government awarded Colonel Townsend £40,000. compensation, a huge sum in those days.

Story tells us further that, in May, 1691, Colonel Townsend (who died in 1692 and is buried in the Townsend tomb in the ruined Church in Castlehaven cemetery) sent a party of his militia men, stationed at Castlehaven Castle, to scour the country. On the way they met a party of rapparees and killed their Captain Regan and Borg, his Lieutenant, and four others.

From Ensign Crammond's Diary of 1690/1691, in the British Museum, we get the following items:-

"On 17th November I went with a small party to Castlehaven, and about the 6th or 7th December I went with a party to the Island of Innisturcean which I put under contribution. December 15th I took a prey of 100 head of black cattle and 25 garrons out of the enemies quarters which I brought to Castlehaven with

*some difficulty. 1691 January 9th Captain Hamilton
and I (then at Bandon) went along with a party to
Clonakilty and 10th to Castlehaven. At the Leap the
enemy laid an ambush for us but we beat them from it
without loss; an ensign of ours was slightly wounded".*

We now meet our old friend Colonel Becher back in
West Carbery, because the document of 1700 already quoted
tells us that after the surrender of Cork in September 1690
the Colonel "with a party of his tenants and others entered
on the Island of Sherkey and there fortified and maintained
a garrison for His Majesty's service and the security of the
protestants of the country". From another source we learn
that Becher received 10/— per day while Governor of Sherkin.

It will be remembered that Dunalong is still locally
known as "the Garrison". Of that garrison Dive Downes, the
Protestant Bishop of Cork and Ross, who visited Sherkin on
14th August, 1699, tells us that "the castle is in the east side
of the island; it is strong, having 2 or 3 platforms for guns
towards the sea whereon are about 8 planted. There is
another platform for guns near the south side of the island.
There are barracks in the castle, and also near the other
platforms, sufficient for a Company of foot". On the
Ordnance Map there is a spot marked "gun point", which is
at the mouth of the harbour just opposite the Beacon, which
is probably the site of the south platform referred to by the
Bishop. He also tells us that at that time Dermot O'Driscoll
was "Popish Priest of the Parishes of Creagh, Tullagh and the
Islands".

In July 1691 we hear of Colonel Becher in action, when
400 Jacobites attacked Skibbereen, but were routed, with the
loss of 60 men and a large number of cattle, near the town,
by 500 militia men under the Colonel's command. On that
occasion it is said that he nearly surprised McCarthy Reagh
and Colonel O'Donovan who were not far away.

Becher must have had an extensive roving commission at

that time, for it is related of him that he recaptured a Dutch ship from the Irish in Bantry Bay, when we are told that, besides those killed in the struggle, 30 of the enemy who leapt overboard were drowned before they could reach the shore.

He made his Will in 1705, and charged his estate with an annuity of £9.4.7. to be paid to the Protestant Church of the Parish of Ballymodan, Bandon, so evidently he did not forget the association of his family with Bandon. This annuity continued to be paid up to the year 1931 when it was redeemed under the Land Acts.

The Colonel died in 1709, and is buried in Aughadown where his tomb can still be seen in the South West corner of the older section of the graveyard. The inscription on it reads "Here lyeth the body of Colonel Thomas Becher eminent for justice and love of his country". His age is given as 69. The date of death is damaged but looks like 10th October, 1709. It is of interest to mention here that Aughadown Protestant Church has a communion cup, made between 1706 and 1708, which was presented by Mrs. Elizabeth Becher, who probably was the Colonel's wife. Also, that Smith, in his History of Cork, written about 1750, states that Aughadown was the seat of Colonel Becher, and that near the house, on rising ground, was a round tower with a lanthorn on its top. The ruins of these buildings still exist.

The end of the year 1691 saw the end of the fighting, but during that year we are told that vast numbers of Scotchmen following King William's Army, and bought the prey of cattle for about 10/- each, which they then retailed in Dublin and elsewhere for about £3. each, and so disappeared most of the cattle of Munster.

The country must have remained very unsettled for a long time after the fighting ceased, because it is recorded that, in 1694, 40 tories entered Skibbereen, killed two Revenue Officers, and plundered the Customs House, for which Dermot O'Leary and others were proclaimed by the Lords Justices. These tories (also called rapparees) were dispossessed young men who were outlawed, and who went in bands round the country living as best they could, and plundering the settlers when the opportunity arose.

Daniel O'Donovan of Bawnlahan, already mentioned, got himself into trouble during the period with which we are dealing. First, in 1684, being then a Colonel, he was committed by Sir Emanuel Moore (who married a daughter of Sir William Hull, and who in 1667 got a Patent for Dunmanus and parts of Killeens and Clounties) on a charge of treason for conspiring the King's death at Whitehall, but he was acquitted. In 1689 he was M.P. for Baltimore. In October 1690 he was Deputy Governor of Charles Fort, Kinsale, which, after a fight, he surrendered to the Duke of Marlborough. In 1691 he was ordered to go to Cork and embark but there is a Permit extant, dated 4th January, 1692 signed by "B. Townsend" (son of the Colonel) for Colonel O'Donovan to travel to Timoleague to deliver himself a prisoner to the High Sheriff. He lived till about 1703. His wife was Victoria Coppinger (sister of Domenick Junior) and their daughter, Victoria, married Captain Cornelius O'Donovan, and they were ancestors of Colonel the O'Donovan formerly of Lissard, Skibbereen.

Before closing this chapter we quote the following interesting information recorded in the Journal of Captain John Stevens, an officer in the Army of King James. He says he landed in Bantry on 12th May, 1689 and that "Bantry is a miserable poore place, not worthy the name of a town, having not above 7 or 8 little houses, the rest very mean cottages". From Bantry he marched through Dunmanway and Bandon to Cork, and then to Dublin. He tells us that private soldiers in the Jacobite army received 4/- per week, and Lieutenants 14/-, while Captains got 5/- per day. The brass money issued by King James fell so low in value that

5/- of it was required to buy a loaf of bread similar to those sold in London for one penny. The Captain says he paid £5. for a pair of shoes, and a suit of clothes cost him £18. When even the brass money got scarce the Army got no pay. This brass coinage was suggested by a Scotchman, but the native Irish bore practically the entire loss.

From the Captain's remarks about Bantry we must conclude either that that town was founded later than Skibbereen, or else grew more slowly, because the account of Bishop Dive Downes, who visited Skibbereen, and preached there on 13th August, 1699, suggests that Skibbereen was then a substantial town.

CHAPTER XII

AFTERMATH OF THE WAR

After the war the usual attainders, confiscations, and emigration began. The Becher document of 1700 records that the Colonel's old enemy Cornelius O'Driscoll had been attainted of High Treason. From another source we learn that Cornelius O'Driscoll Junior, and 8 other O'Driscolls, were attainted. Cornelius Junior went to Spain and became a Lieutenant-Colonel in Count Daniel O'Mahony's regiment of dragoons.

Walter and Edward (or Edmund) Galwey, who then owned Baltimore, were attainted and lost their property.

Walter Coppinger (son of Domenick deceased) was outlawed in 1691 for High Treason at Mallow on 1st May, 1690. In 1694 there was an Inquisition on his property, taken in the Kings Old Castle, Cork, (which then stood beside the Queen's Old Castle, and the two at one time formed a water gateway). Thomas Becher of Aughadown (presumably the Colonel) was one of the Jurors at this Inquisition. Some of Walter's lands are set out, including Gortnahorna, Lissapooka, Rincolisky, East Inishkeame and Hare Island. In the Coppinger Family History it is stated that the outlawry of Walter ruined the family.

Walter's son, Domenick Junior, married Colonel Townsend's daughter, Dorothea, as previously mentioned. He died before his father was outlawed. He made his Will in 1688 and appointed his father guardian of his son James, and gave his father his four Courts of Baltimore, Cloghane, Kilfinnan and Rincolisky. The only mention of the testator's wife in the Will is that she was to see the doctor paid and give him the grey mare!

In some books it is stated that the testator's son James was also outlawed, and that he never got back any of this lands, but the documents we shall quote later seem to contradict these statements. It is on record that on 13th July, 1700 he presented a Petition to the Chichester House officials claiming Derryleigh, Cullenagh, Shreelane, Gortamucklagh and Drummig, which had been mortgaged by his father to Edward Galwey who had been outlawed, but the Petition was dismissed. This James had an uncle of the same name (brother of Domenick Junior) who was outlawed and went to France, and perhaps the writers of the books mentioned above may have confused the two names?

In 1698 an Act was passed to deal with the sale of forfeited estates, and a new Court of Claims was established with Trustees of Claims to operate therein. Human nature appears in an ugly light when there is loot to be obtained, and the scramble for money, cattle and land seems to have produced much dishonesty, bribery and corruption amongst high and low, gentle and simple. Commissioners were appointed to enquire into the dealings with the confiscated property in Ireland, and they issued their Report on 15th December, 1699 which for courage and candour can hardly be surpassed. They stated a million acres had been confiscated and the following are a few of the irregularities they found.

1. Officials illegally collected fees from claimants. For example, the Registrar, Palmer, took £86. from Luke Dillon when his father's estate was restored to him, and not to be outdone the Crier, Steel, took another £15. from poor Dillon.

2. Pardons were illegally bought. For example, Lord Bellew gave Lord Raby £1000. for his influence with the King to obtain a pardon.

3. Large grants of land were made to nobles and others for services rendered during the war.

4. Officials who took possession of flocks valued them too low. For example, horses were valued at 20/- and a

sheep at 2/6d. and then sold to friends.

5. Even those in the highest offices misbehaved. For example, Lord Connigsby (a Lord Justice) seized 300 head of horned cattle, and several horses, and the valuable plate of the Mayor of Dublin and never accounted for same. And the Clerks of the Revenue delivered great quantities of valuable effects to Major-General Kirk, and others, not accounted for.

6. The officers of the Army pillaged.

7. Trees in County Kerry, to the value of £20,000. were cut or destroyed. Large trees were sold for 6d. each, so greedy were the speculators. Even Sir John Hely, Chief Justice of Common Pleas, was cutting down all the avenues and groves round the Castle, near Dublin, he had bought from Lord Conigsby.

8. Several obscure persons, who owned nothing before the war, were then masters of large estates, seized by intrigue or collusion.

9. Sales of property were made only in Dublin, so bidders were very limited, and those in the swim bought them in cheap. Thomas Broderick, a Privy Councillor and Inspector of Auctions, was specially named as having bought huge estates in partnership with William Connelly.

10. Receivers and Commissioners of Revenue bought under borrowed names. For example, Mr. Culliford, under the name of Fernley, seized upon several estates for the King, which he afterwards appropriated to his own use.

11. Estates were let on leases at an undervalue in rent without being put up for sale.

Whether this Report produced prosecutions against those named, or whether such persons challenged the Commissioners to duels, or whether the whole system was reformed, we do not know, but the Trustees continued to sit at Chichester House, Dublin, and, as previously stated, the Decree issued to Colonel Becher (therein described as of "Sherkin") on 16th September, 1700 is still in existence. In it are set out the facts already recited, and then the Commissioners found that the Agreement entered into between Becher and Cornelius O'Driscoll was made under duress and that, owing to the attainder of O'Driscoll, the lands claimed were not vested in the Trustees. They therefore allowed Becher's claim to the lands. Cornelius O'Driscoll was not, of course, present or represented at the hearing being then, no doubt, "on the run".

Meantime, the sales of confiscated lands continued, and in 1703 "the Governor & Company for making hollow sword blades", a speculating Company, bought many lands in West Carbery, including "the castle, town and lands of Bally-mac-Rowan" (Ballymacrown) and Cloghanemore, which included Lissangle and Cloghan Castle thereon, also "Lissalogherrigg" which included Derrylugga and Inchinagotagh. The advertisement for sale of Cloghanemore stated the lands were 2 miles from the Church and Market of Skibbereen, and the tenant's name was then Robert Atkins. In Cromwell's time Cloghan Castle was stated in the Down Survey to be roofed, but it is not mentioned in 1703 so must then have been in ruins. Later in the same century we find the Newman family the owners of Cloghanemore, and other adjoining lands, including Betsboro House, no doubt purchased from the above Company.

In 1703 also the Galwey forfeited estate at Baltimore was sold for £1809 to Percy Freke of Rathbarry (Castlefreke), who was an ancestor of the present Lord Carbery. Freke sat as M.P. for Baltimore the same year. A semicircle of stones sunk in the public road in Baltimore, opposite the gate leading to the ruined Coastguard Station, is said to mark the front step of Freke's house. The property purchased remained in the ownership of the Carbery family up to the year 1919 when it was sold.

Amongst other claimants in 1700 was the Archbishop of Dublin, who claimed and was allowed part of the O'Driscoll Estate. Ardraly was apparently included in this Grant, as it certainly belonged to the Protestant Church authorities up to about 75 years ago when it was sold.

As regards James Coppinger, who married Sarah Baily in 1699, and, secondly, Anne Youd in 1718, we must now mention some documents which are not easy to reconcile with the statement of some writers that all his lands were confiscated and not returned to him, nor yet with the fact that Cloghan was sold in 1703.

The first document to be mentioned is a Lease made in 1705 by James Coppinger to John Cole of 10 gueeves of Inane (Reenarogy), for 999 years, at the yearly rent of £2. Coppinger is described as of Castle — — but unfortunately, the parchment is damaged here, and the missing word cannot be read, but it did not contain more than 5 letters, and it ended with "e", so the word may have been "Inane". This Lease was always treated as valid, and the rent was paid up to 1931, when it was redeemed under the Land Acts, but the Bechers were the owners of the rent from 1746. Inane cannot have been confiscated about 1700 or the Lease would not have been recognised.

The second document is a Latin copy, with an English translation, of a "Fine", which was an ancient method of conveying land abolished in 1834. Under this method of conveyancing a Court Case was brought, and 4 Proclamations had to be made. The first of these in the case in question, is dated 28th November 1710, and the last 20th June, 1711. The suit was between Ralph Freke (son of Percy Freke) of Castlefreke, Plaintiff, and James Coppinger of Rincolisky (son and heir of Domenick Coppinger late of Lisapooky), and Sarah (born Baily) his wife, Defendants. Judgment was given for the Plaintiff, who paid the Defendants £1829, and they quitted claim to the Plaintiff for ever. The lands mentioned were "the Manor of Baltymore otherwise Oldcourt, the Manor of Gortnehorne otherwise Kilfineene, the Manor of Cloghane and the Manor of Rinecolisky" with 2 castles (probably Kilfinnan and Rincolisky) and 1000 acres of land and more of pasture, furze etc. A number of townlands are also named running from Cregg (near Coppingers Court) to Coolbane (Caheragh) and Lackaghane (Baltimore). A large number of small chief rents are also set out, payable out of townlands very widely scattered. Many of these are near Skibbereen, such as Bunalun, Maulbrack, Lahertidaly and Rea. The Carbery Estate continued to collect these Chief Rents up to recent years, when nearly all of them have been redeemed under the Land Acts. It is hard to believe that a proceeding like this would have been entertained by the Court unless James Coppinger still had some interest in the lands in 1710, and was not an outlaw liable to be killed at sight.

On the other hand, we find that on 28th February, 1698 Colonel Becher made a Lease to James Coppinger of the lands of Kilfinnan, Rouryglen and Kileenleagh for 999 years at a rent of £60.10.0. and the Bechers continued to collect this rent up to a few years ago when it was redeemed under the Land Acts.

The next document to be noted is dated 20th March, 1698 and is also a Lease for 999 years, made by John Leslie to James Coppinger, of Hare Island and East Skeam, Corravoley, Lissaclarig and Morahin in West Carbery, and Gurtachorna, Lissapooka, and other lands in East Carbery, at the yearly rent of £145. This is followed by a sub-Lease, dated 27th July, 1716, made by Michael Becher (presumably the Colonel's son), Richard Townsend (presumably an uncle of Coppinger), who are described as the Representatives of Coppinger, to Bryan Townsend (his uncle) of the East Carbery lands, at the yearly rent of £169. This document does not state that Coppinger was then dead or incapacitated, nor does it give any reason why James should not have made it himself. These two Leases remained in force for over two centuries, and were recognised in 1854 when the Incumbered Estates Court sold part of the lands comprised therein.

It will be seen that Hare Island, Gurtnehorna and Lisapooka are included in this Lease from Leslie, though previously same were owned by the Coppingers. It seems probable that these lands were forfeited and granted to Leslie, who then demised to James Coppinger. No doubt the same applies to Kilfinnan etc. acquired by Colonel Becher, and leased by him to Coppinger as already stated. It looks as if Coppinger was on very friendly terms with the new owners or they would not have granted him these long Leases.

But if James Coppinger was outlawed in 1691, as claimed, he surely would not have been acquiring property in 1698, and making a Lease in 1705. It is clear that he was not the fee simple owner of Kilfinnan or Cloghane in 1710/1711, yet he seems to have purported to sell these lands with others to Ralph Freke. It is difficult to explain this, but, perhaps, the solution is that Freke took a chance and bought all that Coppinger had got back, or might hope to get back, and the small price paid seems to corroborate this. No reference to Coppinger's leases is made in the Fine to Freke.

But the Coppinger star, which had been shining in West Carbery for a century, was now setting, and, though Dr. William Coppinger was Roman Catholic Bishop of Cloyne and Ross in 1827, the last we hear of the family locally is that, less than a century ago, they had a corn store at the rear of Townshend Street, Skibbereen, with an entrance through the lane still bearing their name, and that some of them are buried in the Abbey, Skibbereen, where their head stone can still be seen.

Another family which seems to have acquired large

estates in West Carbery at this time is that of Tonson. Major Richard Tonson was the first to arrive, and he obtained a Grant from Charles II for his services during the Civil War, and he purchased "the castle and lands of Spanish Island". He married Elizabeth, a sister of his neighbour, Colonel Becher, and their daughter, Elizabeth, married Colonel Daniel Donovan of Bawnlahan, M.P. in 1689. The Major died in 1693, and his son and heir, Henry, of Spanish Island, married a daughter of Sir Richard Hull, Judge of the Court of Common Pleas in Ireland, who was a son of Sir William Hull already mentioned. It was Henry Tonson, then of Newcourt, who built the wall round that estate. He died in 1703, and was buried in Aughadown, where his tomb can still be seen. The flat cap stone has the unusual feature of having two inscriptions to him. The first and principal one runs east and west and reads: "Here lyes the body of Captn. Henry Tonson who departed this life November the twenty fifth and in the thirtyeth seventh year of his age 1703". The 2nd one which is damaged, runs north and south and reads: "The 25 of Ober interred — Captn. H. T's body the 37th year 1703".

His son, Richard, described in different documents as of Spanish Island, Bridgetown, and Dunkettle (near Cork) married the widow of Michael Becher of Aughadown, and he was M.P. for Baltimore in 1727, and held that position for 46 years until his death in 1773. He devised his estate to his illegitimate son Colonel William Hull, provided he took the name of Tonson, which he did, and in 1783 he became Baron Riversdale of Rathcormac, and he married one of the Bernards of Bandon. He died in 1787, and his son, the 2nd Baron, died in 1848 without issue. He was succeeded by his brother Dr. Ludlow Tonson, Protestant Bishop of Killaloe, who died in 1861, unmarried, when the title became extinct. Most of the Riversdale Estate in West Carbery was sold in the lifetime of the 2nd Baron, including lands round Ballydehob, Caheragh and Drimoleague.

The Somerville family came to Ireland from Scotland in 1690 when Rev. Wm. Somerville settled in Ulster, flying from religious persecution in Scotland. In 1732 his son Thomas Somerville, who was educated in Dublin, became a clergyman at Myross and Castlehaven, and in the course of time, the family acquired a considerable estate in that locality. There is a very large Somerville tomb in Castlehaven graveyard, built by the son of Thomas known as "Tom the Merchant", who died in 1793.

The Coghill family settled in Ireland during the reign of Charles II.

The Swantons are still another family which must have arrived in West Carbery about this time, as we are told that Swanton was a Williamite arrival in Bandon about 1690. During the following century the family acquired large estates, and founded the town of Ballydehob, which at one time was called "Swantons Town". In 1768 Richard Tonson demised lands, in and near Ballydehob, to William Swanton for lives, renewable for ever, which suggests the two families were then on very good terms. A William Swanton made his Will in 1825, and refers therein to property owned or rented by him in over 70 different townlands, mainly round Bally-dehob, but extending westerly to Goleen, Dunmanus and Durrus, and easterly round Skibbereen and beyond Leap.

It would be difficult to trace, and tedious to record, all the persons who flocked into West Carbery between 1600 and 1800, but it would appear that, during that time, three of the great tribes viz:- the McCarthys, O'Driscolls, and O'Mahonys, entirely disappeared as landowners. The O'Don-ovans, however, seem to have succeeded in retaining, or getting back, some of their lands, for, in 1746, we find Daniel O'Donovan (a grandson of Daniel already mentioned), of Bawnlahan, making a lease of Derryclogh (near Drim-oleague). This Daniel, at the age of 60, being then a widower, married Jane Becher, aged 15, by whom he had 4 children!

He must have been very proud of his young wife, because he changed the name of Bawnalahan to Castle Jane, a name which has long since been forgotten. He was buried in Myross in 1778, as was also his wife in 1812, both in the O'Donovan tomb, built in the form of a pyramid. We also find a Morgan O'Donovan, in 1748, making a lease of Barna (Caheragh). Besides these, The O'Donovan, of Lissard, owned a good deal of land in the neighbourhood of Skibbereen which, in recent years, was sold under the Land Acts, and to other purchasers.

It is commonly said that a slow building up lasts longer than a mushroom growth, and also that no man values what he gets for nothing. These remarks seem to apply to these settlers all over Ireland, for many of them, or their successors, piled up such debts and mortgages about a century after their arrival that an Act had to be passed, in the year 1850, establishing a special court to deal with the sale of incumbered estates in Ireland, known as the Incumbered Estates Court, which was afterwards replaced by the Landed Estates Court, and later still by the Land Judges Court. A large number of estates in West Carbery were sold by those Courts, which brought in a new crowd of landowners, who were eventually compulsorily bought out under the recent Land Acts.

The oldest family of the settlers, who also retained their estates the longest, are the Bechers, as they kept a large part of their property until 1931, when the agricultural portion was acquired by the Land Commission under the Land Acts, but the Bechers still own a considerable section of Skibbereen town. This family, at the beginning of the 19th century, had enormous estates in West Carbery, running from Kilfinnan (Glandore) to the Mizzen Head, and nearly to Bantry. The Creagh branch owned about 11,000 acres, most of it between Skibbereen and Baltimore, including the islands of Cape Clear, Sherkin and Ringarogy. This estate was then the property of William Wrixon, (whose father had married Mary

Becher). He took the surname of Becher and was created a
Baronet in 1831. The Hollybrook branch owned about
17,000. acres, much of the estate being round Aughadown,
but extending to Dunmanus, and beyond Goleen. This
estate was sold in the Incumbered Estates Court about 1853,
the owner being then Richard Henry Hedges Becher.

Before leaving the subject of the Bechers, let us relate
the romantic marriage of the Colonel's daughter, Elizabeth,
to Horatio Townsend, Captain of the War Sloop, "Lynn",
who was a son of Colonel Townsend. It appears that Horatio
landed one day on Sherkin, and, on his way to visit the
Bechers at Dunalong, he saw Mrs. Becher combing the long
hair of her fair daughter, Elizabeth. It was a case of love at
first sight, but as he was only the fourth son, and had poor
prospects, his suit was not welcomed, but persistence succeeded, and he married her. He died of fever on his ship soon
after, leaving his wife with one daughter, and whatever property he possessed. His widow was soon consoled as, in 1701,
she married Bishop Dive Downes, who, 2 years before, as
already mentioned, had visited Sherkin and, no doubt, met
the lady of the occasion. The Bishop was married 4 times,
the widow Townsend being the third wife.

Before closing this Chapter it is of interest to mention
that it was on 30th April, 1697 H.M.S. "Loo", during a gale,
was wrecked on the rock at the mouth of Baltimore Harbour,
since when it is known as the Loo Rock, on which there is
now a buoy.

Forged and fradulent Deeds must have been very
common during the 17th Century, for, in 1707, an Act was
passed establishing a Registry of Deeds in Dublin which is
still operating. The Preamble to the Act states that its
object was to secure purchasers, and prevent forgeries and
fraudulent gifts, and it then naively adds that same were
"frequently practised in this Kingdom, especially by papists,
to the great prejudice of the Protestant interest thereof".

CHAPTER XIII

THE 18th TO THE 20th CENTURY

After the close of the hectic 17th Century, and the disposal of the lands confiscated during the Williamite war, Carbery seems to have passed into a subdued and comparatively peaceful condition, probably due to the fact that most of the chief and fighting men had become "Wild Geese", and had emigrated to the Continent, and also, no doubt, to the very harsh Penal Laws that were passed. Accordingly, only scrappy and not very exciting local items are available for us to tell in this chapter.

In the first place let us relate a story which, while it does not actually touch West Carbery, connects Bandon with the English Royal Family. William III died in 1702, his wife, Mary, having predeceased him. He was succeeded by Mary's sister Anne, both of them being daughters of James II, by his first wife, who was the daughter of Lord Chancellor Hyde. The following romantic story is told about Hyde and his wife. It appears the wife started life as a bar-maid in Bandon, and proved so satisfactory that when her mistress died her master married her. He died soon after leaving his widow (the ex-bar-maid) very well off. She went to Cork to consult a lawyer about her affairs, and consulted Hyde who was then a young barrister practising in the City. Whether he fell in love with herself, or her brains, or her property, is not recorded, but he married her, and the union proved most satisfactory as he became a Peer and Lord High Chancellor of England, and she became a Peeress and the mother-in-law of a King of England, James II, and the grandmother of two Queens of England, Mary and Anne.

In 1704, by Statute, the Roman Catholic clergy in Ireland were registered. They numbered 1080, of whom 62 belonged to the County and City of Cork.

The 18th to the 20th Century

The last wolf in Co. Cork was killed in 1710, near Kilcrea Abbey, it is said by Bryan Townsend, son of the Colonel.

In 1723 the famous Dean Swift spent the summer in a house outside Union Hall, and it is said that he wrote *Carberiae Rupes* when sheltering from the rain in the Castletownshend demesne still known as "Swift's Tower".

In 1749 a regular post was established between Cork and Skibbereen. The postman went on foot and was paid the princely salary of £6. per year.

In 1796 it was feared the French fleet would enter Castletownshend Harbour, and Richard Boyle Townsend prepared to resist them and fortified Castletownshend, but the foggy weather veiled the Harbour, and the French went on to Bantry Bay, arriving there on 22nd December and leaving on 5th January, 1797.

On the news of their arrival reaching Cork (per Mr. White, afterwards Lord Bantry), it was Commander John Townsend who volunteered to sail to Bristol to inform the English authorities, and he did so in the teeth of the gale which scattered the French fleet and stopped the invasion.

Needless to say there was great excitement when the French fleet was first sighted by local fishermen, and, while the men watched events along the coast, the women were rushed off to Cork and Bandon, or to the Kerry hills, and the local yeomanry were mobilised, and Bantry was occupied by English and Irish troops. Richard White, of Seafield, sent a boat with 10 boatmen to one of the French ships, with a letter asking who they were, but the boat and crew were retained and did not return. A French long boat, with an officer and crew, put off from one of the ships, but was driven ashore on Bere Island and captured. This boat remained in a house on the Bantry Estate up to a year or two ago when it was sent to the Dublin museum. During their stay, the French plundered and then sank a Guinea trader sheltering in

93

the bay, but they allowed the crew to go ashore in a boat, and this seems to have been the only hostile act they committed. It was immediately after this that the Signal Tower was erected in Cape Clear and others were put up round the coast, such as at Spain and Toehead, all being in sight of each other, in order to signal prompt warning of any other invasion.

About 1785 was built the mill at Rineen (the first of its kind in Carbery), which was soon after followed by that at Lurriga erected by Messrs. Samuel T. Wright and Clerke, and another at Leap which was built by Messrs. Jervois of Brade. But there was an older mill at Lurriga, as in his Will, made in 1692, Colonel Townsend specially mentions the mill and salmon fishing on that townland.

In 1770 block wheels were first introduced into West Cork. They were made of sold blocks of timber, about 3½ feet in diameter, and from 6 to 8 inches thick, and they were heavily bound all round with iron.

The famous Rebellion of 1798, in County Wexford, produced no fighting of note in West Carbery, but it caused the quartering of military and yeomanry. The last generation used to relate stories, told to them by their parents, of the atrocities of the yeomanry, and that on a rumour of their coming the girls were promptly removed to a place of safety.

In the Parish of Aughadown there was no quartering or disturbance, thanks to the joint efforts of the High Sheriff, Samuel Townsend of Whitehall, the Parish Priest, and the Protestant Rector, who jointly guaranteed the peace of the Parish.

Sir John Freke of Baltimore was at this time Deputy Governor of County Cork. This Rebellion, as usual, was betrayed in advance to the authorities by two men, Thomas Reynolds and Francis Magan.

Towards the end of the 18th century an African trading ship, with a cargo of gold, feathers and ivory, looking for

Crookhaven Harbour, was lured on to the rocks at Castle Island by local people, who burned a light on the old castle on the island. The cargo was looted but the crew got to Baltimore.

The Whiteboy disturbances, which started in 1761, continued off and on into the 19th Century. These Whiteboys were so called from wearing white shirts over their clothes when out on their nocturnal rounds. Their prime object was, by terrorism, to reduce the tithes collected for the upkeep of the Protestant clergy, including the impropriate tithes which had passed into the ownership of laymen after the dissolution of monasteries by Henry VIII. These tithes were originally collected in kind, and consisted of one tenth of the produce of farms, but later the tithes were valued and paid in cash. Eventually Statutes were passed, commencing in 1823, by which the tithes were varied and reduced periodically and now, as already stated, most of them have been redeemed under the Land Acts.

On 22nd of June, 1823 tithe riots occurred at Traligagh, when the police and people fought over 5 sheep seized for non-payment of a tithe of 5/-. Eventually the sheep were sold for 5/- to the Castlehaven clergyman Rev. Robert Morrit. There was loss of life on both sides, a policeman and his driver having been killed of the Government party, and a local man, Jack Regan, who had nothing to say to the riot, was shot by the police. He is buried in Castlehaven graveyard where his name can be read on a tombstone. It is claimed that these riots materially helped to pass the amending Statute the same year.

Samuel Townsend, of Whitehall, obtained permission from the Government to raise a troop of yeomanry cavalry to deal with the local Whiteboy disturbances and he was appointed Captain-Commandant, and the troop was supplied with arms. This troop functioned for two years, and then the Government disbanded it, and the arms were stacked in

Whitehall House. The country again became unsettled, and Townsend, failing to get a convoy to take away the arms, and fearing they would be seized locally, threw the lot into the sea near his house.

About the same time there was another yeomanry, or volunteer, corps, accepted by the Government, in the Baltimore area. It was composed of two companies, having 2 subalterns, 5 sergeants, 1 drummer or trumpeter, and 100 rank and file. Sir John Freke was Captain-Commandant, and Percy Freke and George F. Evans were Captains. Medals were issued, and on one of these, on the obverse, are inscribed the words "Baltimore (Cork) Legion. Presented by Sir John Freke, Captain-Commandant, to John Warren, 1804".

The country seems to have still remained very disturbed, becaused in 1836 an Act was passed giving Grand Juries powers to levy money on districts, in order to award compensation to people for malicious damage done to their property, a system which has been continued and broadened down to our own time, though Grand Juries have been abolished since the establishment of the Irish Free State. The members of the Grand Jury were County gentlemen of property, who met a couple of times a year at Assizes in the capital of the County (in Cork for Cork County), and discussed the affairs of the County, and had jurisdiction in criminal cases. There was also, of course, the social side and no doubt, a great deal of good food and drink was consumed on those occasions!

In 1838 the Poor Relief Act was passed, authorising the levying of a Poor Rate, which is still collected, and within a few years following, workhouses were erected in Skibbereen and elsewhere. The farmers and labourers were strongly opposed to paying this rate, and shortly after, when the Rate Collector, under the protection of the police, tried to seize a few head of cattle from some people near Rath Chapel, active opposition was encountered, and the police fired, and 2 men were killed, and 2 were severely wounded. This incident, locally known as the "Battle of Rath" ended the opposition.

In 1815 Bandon was the only Sessions Town for West Carbery legal business, and there was only one Sessions there per year. It was not until about 10 years later that the Skibbereen Court House was built, and Quarter Sessions were established there. But, in 1815, there were still Manorial Courts held locally in several places, including Skibbereen, for the recovery of small debts. At that time, however, the machinery of these Courts must have been very weak, because it was a common practice for creditors to watch for a favourable opportunity and seize and drive off a debtor's horse or cow to a distant part of the country, and hold same until the debt was paid.

The present "mail coach road" from Cork to Skibbereen, via Clonakilty, was not completed before 1816, though under construction 3 years before. George Kingston, of Bandon, was then the overseer. He found that he had to vary the line laid out by Larkin, the engineer, which, at one place, would have run through a boggy place under water in winter. This annoyed Larkin, who accused Kingston of incapacity, mismanagement and fraud, and the dispute went before the Grand Jury on 3 occasions, and lasted 2 years. They acquitted Kingston of wilful extravagance, and fraudulent expenditure, but he was removed as overseer. They, however, approved of Kingston's deviations, and to that extent they found Larkin incompetent.

The direct road from Skibbereen to Bantry was not made until about 10 years later than the Clonakilty road, and the road by the river from Skibbereen to Newcourt, and thence to Aughadown, Ballydehob and Rock Island was made about the same time. It seems probable that the "New Bridge" over the Ilen River, near Skibbereen, was also constructed about the same time, because Rev. Horatio Townsend, at one time a clergyman in Skibbereen, writing in 1815, mentions "Abbeystrowery Bridge about ½ a mile below the town". No doubt if the present bridge was then constructed he would also have referred to it as the "New Bridge".

Presumably it was when the mail coach road from Ross to Skibbereen was being constructed that the ravine at Leap was bridged, because Smith, writing in 1749, says "at the upper end of Glandore Harbour is a deep and dangerous glen called "The Leap" on both sides of which is the high road from Ross to other parts of West Carbery. The road crosses this Glen, which is here as steep as a flight of stairs, so that few horses but those that are well used to it would attempt it with courage".

It gets the name of "The Leap", or "O'Donovan's Leap", from some man named O'Donovan, who is credited with having made a spectacular jump across the ravine over three centuries ago.

The following account of a duel is interesting, even though it happened outside West Carbery, but, as the Conners owned land near Ballydehob, it may be included. It appears that, in 1826, Daniel Conner, of Manch House, being a Justice of the Peace, insulted Captain Daunt from the Bench, at Ballineen Petty Sessions, in a case of Haly v. the Captain. Daunt retaliated by insulting Conner at a dance in the house of Dr. Hickey, rector of Murragh. The duel was fought on 31st May, 1826 and Daunt was killed. Both Conner and his second, Bernard Beamish, of Palace Anne, were tried for murder at Waterford on 20th March, 1827, before Judge Burton, and both were acquitted.

Another notable local trial took place the same year, at the Cork Summer Assizes, when Rev. William O'Brien was convicted of having fired at the Right Rev. Dr. Collins, (afterwards Bishop of Cloyne and Ross), with intent to kill him, at North Street, Skibbereen. O'Brien was sentenced to death, but was reprieved owing to his insanity. Eventually he committed suicide 2 years later while still in prison.

An interesting character appears on our horizon between the years 1830 and 1832. His name was Thompson, and he was the son of a Cork merchant, and he had lived for some time in France and Belgium. He was a teetotaller, a vegetarian, and a communist, so was a century ahead of his time, and, accordingly, locally he was deemed very eccentric. He planned to found a communistic settlement at Carhoogarriff, near Leap, on the basis of mutual co-operation, united possession, and equality of exertion and enjoyment, a scheme which has since been worked most successfully in districts of England, and elsewhere. He laid the foundations of a row of houses, and built a round tower for himself, but death nullified his scheme. By his Will, he gave all his property upon trust to found a socialist community at Coronea (Skibbereen), according to certain rules laid down in a book he had published. The Will was contested by his sister, and the Court held that the book was immoral, and therefore the bequest was void, so the sister succeeded to the property. Thompson also bequeathed his body to Dr. O'Donovan (father of the author of "Sketches in Carbery) upon trust to string his bones together, and send same to his friend Mrs. Wheeler, and he specially directed that no clergyman should meddle with his funeral. Finally he gave his library to Dr. O'Donovan personally. As usual, the Will was not read till after the funeral, and, though Thompson was looked on locally as an infidel not entitled to Christian burial, his uncle, one of the Whites of Bantry, insisted on the ordinary service, and Rev. Jones of Drombeg therefore officiated. At the funeral a woman protested against an infidel being buried near her friends, but on receiving £1. she withdrew her objection and left the graveyard. She had only travelled 3 fields when she fell and sprained her wrist, which she considered a divine punishment on her for her bargain! The parson was furious when the Will was read, so Dr. O'Donovan exhumed the body, and sent the bones to Mrs.

Wheeler, and collected the library for himself.

Another interesting case is that of Thomas Harrington, who lived, between 1832 and 1838, in one of the small houses, now in ruins, under Ardagh Hill, near Glandore Bridge, and who died there of tuberculosis. For some time before he died it was claimed that lights issued from his body, varying from faint glimmerings to brilliant stars, meteors, balls of fire, etc. The case got widespread notoriety, and was discussed in many newspapers of the time, and people came from far and near to see the phenomena. Dr. O'Donovan, already referred to, examined the case scientifically, and reported to the Dublin Medical Press that on 3 nights out of the 14 he spent with him, he saw a luminous fog, and scintillations, like phosphorus, and he considered they came from the dying man's body. Locally, the case was known as "Harrington's Lights".

In 1843 the celebrated Daniel O'Connell held one of his "monster meetings" on Curragh Hill, Skibbereen, in favour of the repeal of the Union of Ireland with England, and on that occasion he was entertained in the Temperance Hall in Townshend Street, Skibbereen. Bantry sent to the meeting a band in a boat, mounted on wheels, and flying a flag.

On 20th September, 1843 a whale, 72 feet long, got stranded on Rabbit Island (Glandore) and its jaw bones still stand in the grounds of Lissard House, Skibbereen.

We shall reserve an account of the Famine of 1846/7 until the next Chapter.

The Fenian Movement had many adherents in West Carbery. In fact, the first of the Phoenix Clubs, which became revolutionary societies, was founded in Skibbereen, about 1858. The chief organiser of these Societies was James Stephens, ably assisted by Jeremiah O'Donovan Rossa who carried on a business in Skibbereen. Members were secretly drilled, even in the outskirts of the town, but there seems to have been no fighting during the brief rising of 1867. But the citizens were greatly alarmed, and the women and children were sent from the country into the towns for safety. Skibbereen had one anxious night, when it was reported that a a body of armed men were encamped on "Knockaneen" and that they intended to attack the town. Fire arms were handed out by the police to loyal residents, who barricaded their houses, and sat up all night awaiting an attack which never came, and which, perhaps, was not even intended, but the arrival of a troop of lancers the following morning ended the matter, and the armed men on the hill disappeared.

On the east side of the South Harbour, Cape Clear, stood a telegraph station which functioned during the Civil War in the United States of America about 1865. Ships from the States threw the mails into the sea, where they were picked up by boats from South Harbour, and urgent messages were then transmitted from the telegraph station to Sherkin, by submarine cable, and thence, by like cable, from the Abbey Strand (Sherkin) to Baltimore, and thence to London. The station was a ruin as far back as 1876, and, prior to that date, the lighthouse on the hill (built at the beginning of the century) was abandoned, being too high to pierce low fog, and the light was moved to the Fastnet rock.

In 1875, Captain Paul Boyton of the United States of America, in a special life saving apparatus, jumped off an American steamer, 6 miles off the Fastnet, on a stormy night, and, after 7 hours swimming, he landed at Trafraska (Baltimore) with, as he put it, "his boat on his back and paddling his own canoe". He frightened the wits out of the people in the first house he called at, who thought he was the devil, with the strange covering he had on.

The stage coach continued to function in West Carbery up to 1877 when the Ilen Valley Railway to Skibbereen was opened for traffic. The extension to Baltimore did not come until 1893, but the Tramway to Schull started in 1886.

In 1870 Thomas H. Marmion had a coaching

establishment in Bridge Street, Skibbereen. He sent a coach
to Cork each morning (Sundays excepted) at 11.45 a.m. and
a car each day at 4.50 p.m. A 3rd class ticket to Cork cost
5/8d. and a 2nd class one 8/3d.

There was considerable unrest in West Carbery during
the Land League days, which culminated in 1882 in a serious
riot in Skibbereen, following the arrest of Father Murphy of
Schull, and the mob wrecked and looted the shop of John
Copithorne at 5 Bridge Street, and the assistance of the
military had to be obtained to restore order. It was during
this period that the word "boycott" came to get its meaning.
In 1880, Captain Boycott was an agent to Lord Erne, in
County Mayo, and he became so unpopular, and was so
shunned, and therefore "boycotted", that he had to leave.

On the occasion of Queen Victoria's Jubilee, in 1897, a
Skibbereen "humorist", to mark the occasion, hired a hearse
and a car and solemnly staged a mock funeral of the Queen
to the Abbey!

Two other events which occurred during this period
were the night of the Big Wind in January 1839 and the year
of the Great Snow in the spring of 1855.

CHAPTER XIV

FAMINE YEARS

Periodically, Ireland has suffered from famine since potatoes became the staple food of the country, about 1700. For instance, in 1740/41 there was a bad famine and 400,000 people perished. Again, in 1822, the potato crop failed owing to bad weather, and, though there was plenty of grain in the country, because of bad distribution, Skibbereen, in May 1822, was reported to be in a state of distress "horrible beyond description". Typhus and dysentry followed and there were many deaths.

But the famine of 1846/47 has made a deeper impression on us than any of the earlier ones, partly, no doubt, because the older citizens of today knew and conversed with people who had lived through that terrible time and, furthermore, the Skibbereen district was one of the most severely stricken regions in Ireland. Conditions became very bad in the autumn of 1846, with the result that relief works were instituted by the Board of Works and soup kitchens were established in Skibbereen, Baltimore, Sherkin, Cape Clear, Kilcoe, Creagh, Castlehaven, Union Hall, Aughadown, Ballydehob, Schull, Dunmanus, Crookhaven, Caheragh, Durrus, Drimoleague and Drinagh.

There still exists a printed copy of the "Rules for the establishment of a charity soup house in Skibbereen", dated 31st October, 1846, under which a subscription of 1/9d. per month entitled the subscriber to issue 2 tickets per day, giving the holder one pint of soup for each ticket.

On Wednesday, 30th September, 1846, 800 to 1,000 men, employed at Caheragh on relief works, breaking stones on the road, struck work owing to starvation and bad treatment by the official in charge. They marched in formation on Skibbereen, implements on shoulders. The alarmed town shuttered all the shops, and retired to their houses, while Michael Galwey, J.P. mobilised the military in the town, 75 in number, and stationed them under cover of the School in North Street, (built that year), opposite to the Court House. At that time the roads to Cork and Caheragh branched just in front of the Pro-Cathedral, and the Caheragh road ran behind and to the West of the School. Accordingly, the strikers could not see the military until they were about 20 yards away. Galwey ordered his men to load and the strikers halted. He seems to have acted very tactfully, as after some conversation with the men, in which he was assisted by McCarthy Downing M.P., Galwey called for "three cheers for the Queen, and plenty of employment tomorrow" to which the strikers heartily responded. The shops were then reopened, and biscuits were distributed, and after 4 hours the strikers went away.

On 24th October, 1846 Denis McKennedy dropped dead while working on the Caheragh road. At the Inquest, held at the Abbey graveyard, it was proved that, for the week in question, Mrs. McKennedy, for her family of 5, had only 21 lbs. of potatoes (given by a neighbour), 2 pints of flour and one cabbage. Deceased's wages were 8d. per day, and same were in arrear for two weeks, owing to an official error. The Jury found that deceased died of starvation, owing to the gross negligence of the Board of Works, and, unfortunately, this was not the only case of its kind in the Skibbereen district.

Conditions grew steadily worse, though it was claimed that there was Government food stored in Skibbereen which would not be handed out except at a high fixed price. In December, 1846, Dr. O'Donovan, of Skibbereen, reported that he was besieged by applicants for coffins, the shortage of which had become a problem, and that in a house in the Windmill he had seen two bodies which could not be buried for lack of coffins. Eventually, coffins with hinged bottoms were used to carry the corpses to the graves, from which they

North Street, Skibbereen

were dropped into the earth, and the coffins were then ready to bear the next body, which could be repeated indefinitely.

The Doctor also reported that on his way to the Workhouse, about half way, he had found a woman lying in the dyke, paralysed with cold, with a dead child in her arms, and another almost dead clinging to her. She was trying to reach the Workhouse but had collapsed on the way.

People crawled into Skibbereen from the country, in the hope of finding some food, and died there. The Workhouse became overcrowded, and, though built to hold only 800 people, eventually it had 1449 inmates, and then had to be closed against any more. The mortality there was frightful, 140 having died in December 1846 and, early in 1847 (which was a worse year for deaths), there were as many as 65 deaths in one week.

The Skibbereen victims were buried in the Workhouse grounds, in the Old Chapel Yard, and even in the cabins and gardens where they died, but mainly in the Abbey graveyard, where a large plot of ground was reserved for them near the entrance gate, and in front of this the Famine Memorial has been erected, on which have been inscribed the following words:—"Precious in the sight of the Lord is the death of his saints. Ps. CXV—5." "Erected to the memory of those departed ones who fell victims to the awful famine of 1846 and 1847. Eternal rest grant unto them O Lord. And let perpetual light shine on them. May they rest in peace. Amen."

1¼ millions of people died in Ireland during these two years, more than all the service men from the whole British Empire who were killed during either of the two world wars!

There are 2 eyewitness accounts of the famine in our district which are too long to be set out here. The first in contained in a letter, written on 17th December, 1846, by N.M. Cummins, J.P., Cork to the Duke of Wellington, reporting the conditions in South Reen, in the Parish of

Myross (where it is said the first famine death occurred), and begging for official help for the starving people. The other is contained in a pamphlet, entitled "From Oxford to Skibbereen", published in Oxford in 1847, giving an account of a visit to Skibbereen, made that year by Lord Dufferin and the Hon. G.F. Boyle, after which the former subscribed £1,000. to the relief funds.

In conclusion, we may add that Rev. Richard Boyle Townsend, the Protestant Rector of Abbeystrowry, who was interviewed by Lord Dufferin, and who worked manfully to alleviate the distress in Skibbereen, himself fell a victim in the end to the famine fever and died on 7th May, 1850, and received what might be described as a public funeral, so much was he respected by all classes and creeds for his help. And he was not the only one of the helpers who suffered the same fate.

CHAPTER XV

CONCLUSION

And so we end the story of West Carbery at the dawn of the 20th century. That century has only yet run about half its course, and the events which occurred therein are still too fresh to justify recapitulation at present. But, looking backwards, we must admit that during the past half century the conditions of life of the people have materially improved, for they are fed, dressed and housed better, and the reductions in farming outgoings have produced material prosperity for the agricultural population from which all have benefitted, while the Radio, Public Libraries and Cinemas have tended to make life more pleasant.

But what a crowded and stirring half century it has been for us, including 3 wars, viz. the Boer War of 1899-1902, the first World War of 1914-1918, and the second World War of 1939-1945, as well as the Dublin rebellion of 1916, and our successful Revolution of 1920-21, with the subsequent Civil War, all of which have affected West Carbery to some extent.

In civilian pursuits we have seen the coming of aeroplanes, motor cars, and buses, cinemas, and radio, with great improvements in roads and transport and medical science. But, on the other side of the account, life has become much more complex, with Income Tax, and Rationing, and many other Government Regulations and Taxes to contend with, not to mention the dangers of the road from fast transport. However, the hands of the clock cannot be put back, and, whether we like it or not, we must go forward and make the best of life as we find it during the short time we are on this earth.

We have intentionally omitted references to authorities in our story as it is disturbing to find frequent marks in the text pointing to foot notes quoting books where statements can be verified. Instead, we propose now to give a list of the

Conclusion

books which have been consulted before compiling the story. In addition, a number of legal documents have been perused, some of which have been mentioned, and it seems unnecessary to list the others.

BIBLIOGRAPHY

Bennett	History of Bandon
Cusack	History of Cork
Rev. Gibson	History of Cork
Smith	History of Cork
Joyce	History of Ireland
Abbe MacGeoghegan	History of Ireland
Curtis	History of Mediaeval Ireland
Coppinger	History of that family
McCarthy	History of that family
Canon O'Mahony	History of that family
Townshend	History of that family
Somerville	History of that family
Rev. O'Rourke	History of the Famine
O'Brien	The Great Famine
Butler	Gleanings from Irish History
Butler	Confiscations in Irish History
McManus	Irish Cavalcade
Dr. J. O'Donovan	Miscellany of the Celtic Society
Dr. J. O'Donovan	Sketches in Carbery
Rev. Otway	Sketches in Ireland
Prendergast	Cromwellian Settlement
Rev. Murphy	Cromwell in Ireland
Miss Hickson	Ireland in the 17th century
Miss Jacob	United Irishmen
Westropp	Early Maps of Ireland
Westropp	Fortified headlands and castles of South Munster
Moore	Memoirs of Captain Rock
Leask	Irish Castles
Rev. Townsend	Survey of County Cork
Lewis	Topographical Dictionary of Ireland
Rev. Webster	Church Plate
Rev. Webster	Diocese of Cork
Rev. Webster	Diocese of Ross
Ensign Crammond	Diary of 1690
	Pacata Hibernia
	Book of Irish Peerages
	Calendar of Irish Saints
	Cork Historical & Archaeological Journal
	Report of the Commissioners of Public Works

It is proposed to add in subsequent chapters some short
notes on the Castles, Monasteries, Churches, Towns and

Conclusion

Villages of West Carbery, which could not well be given in the foregoing pages without interrupting the course of the Story itself.

Our object has been, in compiling the Story, to give some kind of a connected narrative of affairs in West Carbery during about 2,000 years, from which we can visualise that life there, while far from being ideally peaceful and happy, was not so entirely chaotic as some people would have us believe.

In spite of wars and pestilences and persecutions the Irish Nation has survived, and, better still, in spite of hardships and trials, the Nation's sense of humour has survived, and we can claim with justice that West Cork humour is "a thing of beauty and a joy for ever".

CHAPTER XVI

THE CASTLES OF WEST CARBERY

Nearly all the ancient castles were untenanted and ruinous at the time of the Down Survey (about 1653).

THE O'MAHONY CASTLES

They were 12 in number, viz:— Ardintenant (White Castle), Castle Island (Black Castle), Castle Mehigan, Ballydivlin, Dunlough (Three Castle Head), Dunmanus (built on a Dun), Dunkelly, Dunbeacon, Knockeens, Leamcon, Lissygriffin and Rossbrin. **Dunlough** was the first built, (about 1207); and **Dunmanus** the last, (about 1450), which is also the largest and best constructed. **Ardintenant** was the chief castle. **Rossbrin Castle** was forfeited in 1562 owing to its owner's piracy. **Dunbeacon Castle**, after the Desmond rebellion, was confiscated, but was first burnt by its owner. In 1602 it was purchased by the Great Earl of Cork from Michael Apsley. **Leamcon** and **Dunmanus Castles** were attacked and captured by the English in 1602, but were later returned to their owners.

THE McCARTHY CASTLES

They were 5 in number, viz:— Kilcoe, Cloghan (on Lissangle) and Ballyourane, belonging to Clan Dermod, and Gortnaclohy and Lettertinlish, belonging to McCarthy Reagh as part of his demesne.

Kilcoe Castle is the best preserved one in West Carbery, and possesses an oubliette, or secret vaulted chamber, under the floor of one of the rooms, as well as a quite good drainage system. This was the last castle to fall to the English in 1603. **Lettertinlish** was captured and destroyed the previous year, and both it and **Gortnaclohy Castle** have entirely disappeared for over 200 years. Close to the latter is a small steep hill, still known as Gallows Hill, on which tradition says the

Castle's prisoners were executed.

Cloghan Castle was sold by the McCarthys to Sir Walter Coppinger in 1594. Only the outline of the foundations still remain to be seen and even these are doubtful. There are walls in parts up to 6 ft. high, at **Ballyourane** which the Ordnance Map shows as the Castle though local tradition says they are part of a chapel.

THE O'DRISCOLL CASTLES

O'Driscoll Oge, the chief of Collybeg, had one castle, that of **Rincolisky** (Whitehall), built about 1495. It was taken by the English in 1602 and later became the property of the Coppingers. A considerable portion of the keep still remains. O'Driscoll More, the chief of Collymore, had 8 castles, viz:— Dunasead (Baltimore), Dunalong (Sherkin), Dunanore (Cape Clear), Ardagh, Oldcourt, Donegal (Ringarogy), Cloghan (Lough Hyne) and Castlehaven. **Dunasead** and **Donegal** were built in 1215 by the English for Lord Sleviny (or Slynie) but were taken from the English after the battle of Callan in 1261. **Dunasead** must have been recovered by the English because we are told that in 1305 it was burned and demolished by Donal McCarthy "after he had taken it from the English of Desmond". It suffered the same fate in 1537 from the Waterford men, so the present ruin is not more than 400 years old. The Spaniards occupied it in 1601/2 after which it passed into the possession of the Coppingers. Dunanore was also built in the 13th century.

Some writers say that **Dunalong** (locally known as The Garrison) was built in 1215 by the English and captured by the Irish in 1261. Others say it was built in 1460 by Florence O'Driscoll, who also built Sherkin Abbey the same year. It was damaged by the Waterford men in 1537, and, about a century later, it passed into the ownership of the Bechers, who resided there up to the end of the 18th century.

Donegal Castle has entirely disappeared, save that the site can still be traced, and it is said that a good many of its stones went into the building of the Pro-Cathedral, Skibbereen, in 1826.

Castlehaven collapsed in 1926 and is now a heap of rubble. Old photographs show that it resembled Raheen Castle in structure, so may have been built about the same time. Raheen is said to have been built in 1584.

There are only fragments of the Castles at **Ardagh** and **Cloghan** standing, but the keep, and walls of the courtyard at **Oldcourt** still remain, and this Castle, also known as Creagh Court, was occupied by an O'Driscoll as late as 1700.

Considerable portions of **Dunasead, Dunalong** and **Dunanore** still remain.

THE O'DONOVAN CASTLES

Clan Cahill had three castles, viz:— Castle Donovan, Raheen Castle, and Castle Ire (or Ivor).

It is said that **Castle Donovan** was built, about 1560, by Donnell (I) O'Donovan, and **Raheen Castle**, about 1584, by Donnell (II) O'Donovan. Both were wrecked by Cromwell's men in 1649/50, but the ruins can still be seen.

Castle Ire, of which only a fragment remains, is said to have been built in 1251 by Ivor O'Donovan, who was the son of Cahill the founder of the Sept. There is a legend that Ivor was a celebrated trader, and that every 7th year his ship is seen under full sail on the waters of Lough Cluhir between the Castle and the sea.

Clan Loughlin had Glandore and Kilfinnan Castles, and possibly also Benduff, otherwise Castle Salem, all in East Carbery, though Benduff may have belonged to McCarthy Reagh.

Glandore Castle was built in 1215 by the English for Barrett, but was captured in 1261 by the Irish, and occupied by the O'Donovans. It is still occupied as a residence, as is also

Kilfinnan, both of which have been incorporated into modern houses.

Benduff Castle, portion of which still remains, was built about 1500, it is believed by Katherine (wife of McCarthy Reagh and daughter of the 8th Earl of Desmond who was executed at Drogheda). It is said that her spirit, called "The Black Lady", still haunts the place. This property was confiscated after 1641 and was granted by Charles II to William Morris in 1666. One of his successors was an intimate friend of the celebrated William Penn, the Quaker, who founded the State of Pennsylvania in America.

In the grounds of the Castle is a small but ancient Quaker graveyard, in which even Cork members were buried, the graves running north and south, and with only simple, plain headstones and foot stones to mark them. When William Morris, (grandson of the original Patentee), who died in 1764, was buried there, a rough tomb was erected over him, which so shocked the Quaker sense of propriety that the graveyard was abandoned. But what the Quakers feared to do then has since been done by nature, because the tomb has been wrecked by a tree which has grown up through it!

CASTLETOWNSHEND

There have been several successive buildings erected. The first, a considerable portion of which still remains, was erected by Colonel Townsend, about 1650. It consisted of a dwelling house of two stories, and a small courtyard, all comprised in a square enclosure, with a bastion at each angle pierced with loopholes for musketry, and some openings for small cannon. The ground floor room of the North East bastion has no opening to give any light, so probably it was reserved as a prison or to store ammunition. A larger mansion near by was built later, which was destroyed during the war of 1690, and Colonel Townsend received £40,000. compensation therefor from the Government.

The next mansion fell down when undergoing alteration, and was succeeded by a castle, erected by Richard Boyle Townsend, which was accidentally burnt to the ground in 1852. During the fire, the silver plate, stored in a top room, melted from the heat and flowed down the walls. It was after this that the present castle was built.

AUGHADOWN

Colonel Becher built a mansion here about 1700, on the same general plan as that of Colonel Townsend. The building within living memory was occupied by a caretaker, but has since become a complete ruin, and is rapidly disappearing. Close by are the remains of the building, locally known as the "Gazebo", from which there is a splendid view, and it is said to have been originally covered with glass. There are the remains of a carriage drive from it to the Becher house. Smith, who wrote about 1750, describes the building as a round tower with a lanthorn on its top.

CHAPTER XVII

MONASTERIES AND CHURCHES OF WEST CARBERY

MONASTERIES

There were monastic establishments at **Abbeystrowery** (the Abbey of the Stream) and **Sherkin Island**, both of which were dissolved by Henry VIII. After the dissolution, the property of the Abbeys passed into lay hands. In 1542 a Commission, of which the Earl of Desmond was a member, was appointed "to take inventories of all religious houses in the Counties of Cork, Kerry, Limerick, and Desmond, to dissolve them, and put them in safe custody for the King's use" but many of the friars were not disturbed for years after. Abbeystrowery was a cell to the Cistercian Abbey of St. Mary de Fonte Vivo, and was founded by O'Donovan in

The Castle, Castletownshend

the 13th century, and endowed with 20 ploughlands. Up to recent years, (when most of them were redeemed under the Land Acts), Lay Tithes were payable to the Townshend Estate, out of 20 townlands in the neighbourhood of the Abbey, which probably were those included in the endowment. Three of these townlands, Coronea, Deelish and Mallavonea lie to the South of the River Ilen, and the rest to the North, including Abbeystrowery, Lurriga, Coolnagarrane and Maulbrack. The Abbey building had completely disappeared prior to 1750 when Smith wrote his *History of Cork*. The present ruined Church was erected later than the original Abbey building, and was used as a Parish Church until it became ruinous and was abandoned, and this also happened before 1750 when Smith wrote.

The oldest dated monument in the Abbey Graveyard is an Altar tomb outside of, and to the South of, the ruined church. A translation of the inscription, which is in Latin, reads as follows:— "Pray for me, Daniel McCarthy, priest, who got me made 10th October in the year of Our Lord 1705". Father McCarthy was Parish Priest of Aughadown, Kilcoe and Abbeystrowery, and resided at Coolbane. He was ordained in Dublin in 1668 by Blessed Oliver Plunkett.

There are two Gallwey tombs near by, dated 1714 and 1729. The oldest dated grave stones erected to the memory of members of an existing family in Skibbereen are those of the Crowleys, the earliest date being 1797.

Large numbers of victims of the Famine of 1846/7 are buried in the Abbey, and a monument to them has been erected at the western end of their nameless graves.

Sherkin Abbey, as it is usually called, was built in 1460, by Florence O'Driscoll, as a Franciscan Friary, to accommodate 30 friars. It was in existence for only about three quarters of a century when it was wrecked by the Waterford raiders. The nave is separated from the choir by a tower, 48½ feet high, in which there is a circular staircase leading to the parapet at the top, around which there is only a very low outside wall. Most of the floors in the tower have long since disappeared, leaving a dangerous, internal, welllike deep opening below the parapet, across which a young American, named Gott, jumped some years ago, to the dismay, but not admiration, of his friends, and it is said that the late Canon Goodman of Skibbereen also jumped across it when a young man. This tower was built later than the rest of the Abbey, and it is thought it was erected after, and because of, the Waterford raid. In the adjoining Transept are 2 chapels, with sites for an altar in each, at the eastern end. There are 2 similar sites in the Nave to the west of the tower, and still another at the east end of the choir. The south wall of the choir has three windows under which are recesses for stalls. The north wall of the choir has recesses for two tombs, and there is another of such recesses in the north east angle of the Nave. In the cloister garth an accumulation of debris has been piled in the middle of the quadrangle. The axis of the Church is about 30° to the north of true east.

Sherkin Abbey was dissolved soon after the Waterford raid, and on 6th August, 1578 the property, described as "the site of the house of begging friars of Baltimore with two gardens and a close adjoining", was leased to James Heyden for 21 years at a rent of 26/8d. A similar Lease was made in 1582 to Thomas Wye, and on 4th July 1591 a third Lease was made to John Bealinge for 40 years from the termination of the Lease of 1578. Later, the site became the property of the Becher family, and Lionel Becher of Sherkin used some of the buildings as a curing house for pilchards down to 1769. In 1892 the site was vested by Sir Henry Becher in the Board of Works as an ancient monument. While there is documentary evidence to show that O'Driscoll chiefs and their families were buried in the Abbey the site of their graves is unknown.

Some claim that, at one time, there was another Monastery in

West Carbery, at Carrigillihy in the Parish of Myross, that of
St. Mary de Fonte Vivo already referred to, which others
contend stood at Abbeymahon, near Timoleague, and there
have been several pamphlets written on both sides. It is
agreed that this Abbey was founded in 1172 by Dermot
McCarthy, King of Desmond, but it does seem strange that he
should pass by his own lands in East Carbery and enter the
Parish of Myross then the property of the O'Driscolls, who
were no doubt hostile to him, for the purpose of founding an
Abbey. A further objection is put forward that there is no
graveyard at Carrigillihy, while corpses are still buried in
Abbeymahon. And, lastly, a Church Record of 1694 states
that "Abbeystrowry is an appendix of Abbeymane". On the
other hand Smith, writing in 1750, states emphatically that
the Abbey was not at Abbeymahon, and that extensive ruins
had been discovered in Carrigillihy, with quantities of human
bones, which he said was probably the site. Another modern
writer on the subject has given a third possible solution, viz:—
that originally the Abbey was at Carrigillihy for some
centuries, and that the monks then moved to Abbeymahon
and Carrigillihy was abandoned.

In the Abbé MacGeoghegan's *History of Ireland* it is stated
that the Roches founded a house for Dominicans at **Glandore**
about 1460. If this be correct, could the Carrigillihy ruin be
the remains thereof, or connected therewith? The Ordnance
Map states it is the site of a "Kill". After the dissolution, Sir
Owen McCarthy petitioned Queen Elizabeth for the lands
belonging to the Abbey, but evidently the Petition was
rejected because the lands (including the Abbeystrowry cell)
in 1583 were granted for ever to Sir Nicholas Walsh by the
Queen. Sir Owen died in 1593 and was buried in Timoleague
Abbey not far from Abbeymahon.

There was also a Friary at **Caheragh**, known as "the friary of
the fort", which stood on a high knoll overlooking the
cemetery. It was built in a *lis*.

And, lastly, the Ordnance Map marks the site of a Friary at **Kilkilleen,** where a portion of a wall and mounds of stone remain to show an ancient building, presumably an ecclesiastical one of some sort, as the Decretal Epistle of Innocent III, of the year 1199, mentions that place amongst a number of other Churches in the neighbourhood, including Aughadown, Kilcoe, Schull, Durrus, Drimoleague and Glenbarrahane.

ANCIENT CHURCHES

There are 17 Civil Parishes wholly or partially in West Carbery. Presumably every Parish at one time had its own Parish Church, but some of them have entirely disappeared, such as the original one at Aughadown, which was a ruin as far back as 1699, and is believed to have stood in the centre of the old graveyard. Only fragments of others of these Churches remain, such as that at Castlehaven, which was in bad repair in 1699. All of them became ruins and were abandoned a long time ago. We can only refer here to a few of them.

Abbeystrowery has been mentioned already, and there is no record of any Church in the town of Skibbereen prior to 1686.

Cape Clear Church is known as Kilkieran in commemoration of St. Kieran, who is said to have been born near by in 352, and to have himself carved and erected the stone known as *Gallaun Kieran*, not far from the Church. The present roofless building, which was a ruin as far back as 1693, was erected in the 13th century on the site of an earlier building. After the Reformation it passed into Protestant ownership and became a Parish Church. Rev. Caesar Otway, who visited Schull in 1826, says he stayed with the Protestant Curate of Schull, who told him he was also Vicar of Cape Clear, out of which he received £30, but had no parishioners there except about 20 of the Waterguard, who were Customs men living at

South Harbour, and that he had been inducted in the old Church, then a ruin.

As regards **Creagh**, it is recorded that, in 1544, Henry VIII presented Florence Maghter to the rectory and vicarage of Creagh "the late incumbent being an Irishman". Presumably his Church was the old building (a ruin in 1700) which is close to the Protestant Church still in use at Creagh.

Other ancient Parish Churches, of which considerable portions still remain, are those at **Kilcoe** (a ruin in 1615), **Tullagh** and **Myross**.

There are two other ancient churches of which all records seem to have been lost. One is at Lough Hyne, known as **Templebreedy**, which is very small, and is the most primitive church in the Diocese of Ross. The other, also very small, is on **West Skeam Island**. Around it is a graveyard which is gradually being washed away by the sea, exposing human bones lying a few inches under the soil. In *Sketches in Carbery* it is stated that the name of the Island comes from St. Keam, who lived about the year 400, and was a relative of St. Kieran, but curiously enough no such person appears in the *Calendar of Irish Saints*. The Coppinger Inquisition of 1694 gives the name of the Islands as "Inishkeame", and Bishop Dive Downes, writing in 1699, calls them "East and West Inniskean". Canon O'Mahony says the Islands belonged to the O'Mahonys, and got the name from somebody named "Cian" (a popular O'Mahony name), and that the Islands passed to the O'Driscolls under some marriage settlement between the two tribes.

One other old Protestant Church which may be mentioned here is that at **Brade**, known as Whitechurch, which, while not as old as the others already mentioned, was built in the 18th century. It was dismantled when **Union Hall Church** was built in 1826, and **Leap Church** two years later.

OTHER CHURCHES

Among more modern churches, but in existence now over a century, we have the Roman Catholic **Pro-Cathedral** in **Skibbereen**, built in 1926, at a cost of £3,000. which superseded the Chapel (now disappeared) in Kilmahon graveyard adjoining Chapel Lane, which it is said was built about 1750. The site of the Pro-Cathedral was leased in 1827 by Sir William Wrixon Becher to Dr. Coppinger, then Bishop of Cloyne & Ross, his successor Dr. Collins, and Rev. Jeremiah Moloney P.P. for 999 years at the nominal rent of one peppercorn. The building was considerably enlarged by an addition to the eastern end about 60 years after the Lease. The R.C. Chapel at **Ballydehob** was also built in 1826, and that at **Castlehaven** in 1834, while **Rath Chapel** was built prior to 1837.

The **Episcopal Church** in Skibbereen, which has the rather unusual feature of the congregation facing the West, was built in 1827, at a cost of £1,200. to which the Board of First Fruits made a very substantial contribution. The Church was extended in 1890. First Fruits were the first year's income of every ecclesiastical dignity or benefice, paid by the Appointee to the Pope up to the time of the Reformation, and thereafter to the Crown, up to Queen Anne's reign, when the payments were accumulated for the increase of small livings and the purchase of glebes, and the fund was known as Queen Anne's Bounty. Eventually the funds of the Board were used to build churches and glebes at the beginning of the 19th century. Other Protestant edifices to which the Board contributed are the **Rectory, Skibbereen,** built in 1824, the **Glebe House,** in **Baltimore,** built in 1818, and the **Church** there built the following year, **Creagh Church,** built in 1810, **Aughadown Church** (now a ruin) built in 1812 and **Kilcoe Church** built in 1830, also **Castlehaven Church** built in 1827 and **Ballydehob** and **Caheragh Churches** built in 1829. The Rectories at Creagh and Aughadown were built shortly before 1815, and that at Castlehaven in 1826.

Schull Protestant Church (now a ruin) was built in 1720. Rev. Caesar Otway, who visited it in 1826, describes it as then in use and having a belfry and whitewashed walls. The present **Schull Church** was consecrated in 1854. The Church has a Cup and Paten made in 1694.

The **Skibbereen Methodist Church** was built in 1833, but was reconstructed in 1896.

To conclude this chapter we may add that Ross was created a Diocese by the Synod of Kells in the year 1152, and as a separate Roman Catholic Diocese it continued up to 1748 when it was joined to Cloyne, and it remained so up to the Synod of Thurles in 1851 when it was restored to its original separate position.

The Protestant Diocese of Ross was united to those of Cork & Cloyne in 1583, and has since remained so, save that from 1638 to 1835 Cloyne was a separate Diocese, except for one short period about 1660.

Bishop Lyon already held the See of Ross when Cork & Cloyne were also given to him in 1583. Archbishop Loftus, writing in 1586, stated that Cork & Cloyne were not worth £30. a year to the Bishop, while Ross was of very little value. The Archbishop added that Ross was "in so desolate and barberous a place as is not fit for an Englishman, especially one of his sort (i.e. Bishop Lyon,) to live in". The Bishop had to fly for safety to Cork after 1598, and he reported that church attendance had fallen from 1000 to 5, and communicants from 500 to 3. However, by 1615 he had raised the revenues of Cork & Ross to £200. He died in 1617. His daughter Mary married Henry Becher, presumably the Colonel's son. It was this Bishop who celebrated the marriage of the poet Spenser to Elizabeth Boyle, a relative of the Great Earl of Cork.

CHAPTER XVIII

THE TOWNS AND VILLAGES OF WEST CARBERY

SKIBBEREEN

This, the largest town in the Barony, is said to have been founded after, and as a result of the Algerine Raid on Baltimore in 1631, as the residents of that district determined to settle sufficiently far up the River Ilen to be immune from further sea raids. But it seems likely that at least a hamlet previously existed near the Abbey, and, possibly, there was another near Kilmahon graveyard. But, at any rate, there cannot have been any considerable village or town in existence in 1602 when Carew passed through or, undoubtedly, he would have named it, and garrisoned it. He must have passed through the site of the present town on his way from Dunboy to Lettertinlish Castle, as High Street was the main road to Ross up to the beginning of the 19th century.

In 1666 Charles II granted, by Patent, to Colonel Townsend, certain lands, including Coronea "called by the name of Skubereene", and in 1677 a further Patent was granted to him consolidating all his lands, containing 8000 acres, into "the Manor of Bridgetown, alias Coronea", so there must have been some kind of a town then existing to the West of the Keal.

As regards the rest of the town, to the East of the Keal, this was granted, as "Skibbareen to be for ever called New Stapleton", by another Patent, about 1670 to William Prigg and Samuel Hall. Colonel Becher subsequently acquired portions of this Grant, consisting of North Street and the Northern half of Main Street, while the Estate of Townsend and Wright acquired the rest.

The entire Townsend Estate at Bridgetown, then the property of Mrs. Mundy, was sold in the Land Judges Court in 1897. The Townsend and Wright Estate was partitioned in 1858, and the Wright portion, then the property of Samuel D. Wright, was sold in the Land Judges Court in 1903. Sir William Fane Becher, Bart., and Dr. George H. Townshend still own considerable portions of the town. The tolls of Bridgetown and New Stapleton were also granted to the original Patentees mentioned above, and, eventually, they have been acquired by the Skibbereen Urban District Council, who hold the original of one of the Patents, under the Great Seal, made in 1674, to Prigg and Hall, of the tolls of New Stapleton, and the document is in an excellent state of preservation. The Earl of Orrery (a son of the Great Earl of Cork), who died in 1679, and is buried in St. Mary's Church, Youghal, and who took a prominent part in the fighting in Munster in 1641, acquired the entire Impropriate Tithes of the town, and granted part to the Protestant Vicar for his support, under which Dive Downes, Protestant Bishop of Cork and Ross from 1699 to 1709, tells us that when the man of a family, or a widow, died worth £5. the Vicar had to collect 13/4d. as a mortuary, but, if he was worth less than £5., then his second best suit of clothes, or 6/8d. in lieu thereof. The Bishop also tells us that he preached in Skibbereen on 13th August 1699, and that the Chapel was formerly the Market House, and was consecrated about 1686 by Dr. Wetenhall, (Protestant Bishop of Cork and Ross from 1678 to 1699). That Bishop sat in the Irish Parliament of King James II in 1689, and he did not fly from Ireland, as most of the other Bishops did, and he was in Cork City during the siege by the Duke of Marlborough. In 1698 he had a controversy in Cork with the celebrated William Penn of American fame.

Smith, writing in 1749, says "On the West side of the river is a new erected Church, and in the town a decent Market House". Bennett, in his *History of Bandon*, says the Church was burnt in the reign of James II, but was repaired in 1695

Skibbereen To-day (Aerial photograph by Dr. Daphne D.C. Pochin Mould)

for £20. The Church referred to by Smith, which is on the Long Quay, still exists as a storehouse but has been considerably altered. A graveyard seems to have been near it as, when excavating ground in Bridge Street, some 70 years ago, quantities of bones were dug up and re-interred in the Abbey. It is claimed that the Church referred to by Bishop Downes stood in Mardyke opposite to the present Masonic Hall. The Municipal affairs of the town were managed by Town Commissioners, under the Towns Improvement Act 1854 up to 1st April, 1900, when the town became Urban, since when the Urban District Council functions.

BALTIMORE

This town is said to be the oldest in West Carbery, and to have been a Druidical centre in pre-Christian times. It is well to mention that ordinary towns, as distinct from monastic centres, did not come into being until the 10th and 11th centuries.

Baltimore received a Town Charter on 25th March, 1613, and thereafter returned two Members of Parliament up to the year 1800 when it was disfranchised, and £15,000. was paid by the Government to the Carbery family, the owners of the town, as compensation for the loss of the Charter.

In the Rosscarbery Cathedral there is a book containing a survey of the Carbery Estate made in 1788, and the civic bounds of the township are shown therein. A beacon at the harbour's mouth is also marked.

One of the maps in this book gives the area of the township as 575 acres 2 roods 34 perches, and shows that it was bounded on all sides by the sea, save from Trafraska (then known also as Bruce Cove) to Church Bay. This land boundary followed the road from Trafraska but excluded the glebe land and the old Church (now in ruins). About 10 perches to the West of the by-road leading to the old Church a dot is marked on the map, in the centre of the main road, and over it is written "Limits of the liberties of Baltimore or the Corporation Stone". There is a very large stone, at present in a fence close by, which has been worked, and at some time formed a gate post—can this be the stone referred to?

This map shows 32 lots of property in the township, with the names of the occupiers, the largest land-owner being James Freke, a member of the Carbery family. Amongst the others we find Driscoll, Molloy, Bush and Crowley, whose descendants still remain in Baltimore.

The town seems to have always been a small one as Captain South, writing in 1698 says there were 281 people in it, viz:— 9 seamen, 188 fishermen and 84 boatmen, and there were only 2 Papists!

Smith, writing in 1749, says "Baltimore is now a poor, decayed fishing town with not one tolerable house in it". In Lewis's *Dictionary* of 1837 it is stated that there were then 459 inhabitants, and the road from Skibbereen was called a new one so cannot have been made long before. The history of the old castle has already been fully told.

The town remained the property of the Carbery family from 1703, when it was purchased by Percy Freke, up to 1919 when it was sold. Percy Freke was married to a relative, Eliza Freke, in 1671. Her interesting and amusing Diary has been preserved. One item recorded therein is that before her marriage she lent her husband £10,652.14.10. and after the marriage £11,298. total £21, 950.14.10. in which was included £1,200. lent to him to complete the purchase of Rathbarry (Castlefreke) in 1681 from the Earl of Barrymore.

SCHULL

In ancient times this place was known as Sancta Maria de Scholia, St. Mary of the Schools, which tradition says was the Maynooth of Munster, and that the school was allied to that at Rosscarbery, and stood in South Schull. Bishop Dive

Downes, writing in 1699, says the Schull Church was then unroofed, but he confirmed 40 persons therein. He also says there was no Registrar, no Bible or Book of Common Prayer, and only about 4 Protestant families, and about 400 Roman Catholic families. He says service was held on 3 Sundays per month in a house in Schull, and the 4th in Kilmoe Parish, the Church in which was then in ruins.

Smith, writing in 1749, says "Schull is a small, insignificant village, having few buildings besides the Church and parsonage house".

Lewis's *Dictionary* of 1837 says Schull had then 79 houses and 385 inhabitants.

In the 1699 Rent Roll of the Protestant Diocese of Cork we are told that 9 ploughlands at Schull, with the two Calf Islands, and Crookhaven with the glebe, had been leased to Sir Richard Hall on 21st August, 1663.

DRIMOLEAGUE

Smith's *History* of 1749 says this place was then "a small, inconsiderable village". Its main expansion occurred during the present century.

BALLYDEHOB

This town seems to have been founded towards the end of the 18th century by the Swanton family, and it was at one time known as "Swanton's Town". Smith does not mention it at all, so apparently it did not exist in 1749, but in Lewis's *Dictionary* of 1837 we are told that it had 100 houses and 601 inhabitants, and that "a new line of road, formed by the Board of Works, from Skibbereen to Rock Island runs through it".

CROOKHAVEN

In 1749 Smith says that it was "once a place of some note, but then a small, inconsiderable fishing town". Before the

The Viaduct, Ballydehob

discovery of wireless its harbour was much used by ships, crossing to and from America, calling for sailing orders, but since then the town has greatly decayed, and the harbour is empty. Bishop Dive Downes says there were 200 houses in Crookhaven prior to the rebellion of 1641, but that at his visit, in 1699, there were only 9 Protestant families in the Parish, and about 200 Roman Catholic families.

GOLEEN

This place is not mentioned at all by Smith, so presumably it did not exist in 1749. Probably it owes its existence to the road, made shortly before 1837, from Skibbereen to Rock Island, as being at the head of Crookhaven Harbour, and so much nearer to Schull and Skibbereen, it eclipsed Crookhaven. The Protestant Church at Kilmoe has a cup, made in 1700, with the Arms of Bishop Wetenhall thereon.

CASTLETOWNSHEND

Smith describes it in 1749 as being "a small but well looking village". Presumably it owes its existence to the Townshend family, towards the end of the 17th century.

UNION HALL

It got its name from the Mansion built there, by the Limerick family, in the year 1800, when Ireland became united to England. It cannot have existed long before as Smith does not mention it in 1749.

"THE LEAP"

This place was well known in Carew's time, about 1600, and is described by Smith as being a precipice, so probably the town of Leap did not exist before the ravine was bridged at the beginning of the 19th century, and Lewis's *Dictionary* of 1837 calls it a village.

GLANDORE

This is in East Carbery. It is not mentioned at all by Smith, so must have been a mere hamlet, if it existed at all, in 1749. Even in 1837 Lewis's *Dictionary* calls it a village of 200 inhabitants.

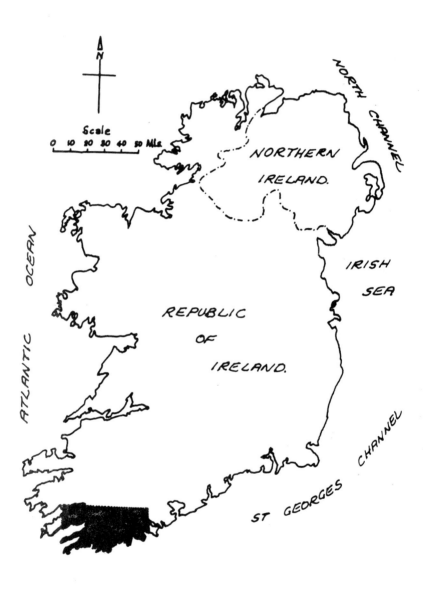

Scale
0 10 20 30 40 50 Mls.

NORTH CHANNEL

NORTHERN
IRELAND.

IRISH
SEA

ATLANTIC OCEAN

REPUBLIC
OF
IRELAND.

ST GEORGES CHANNEL